Hidden Gold

HOW MONTHLY GIVING WILL
build donor loyalty,
boost your organization's income,
and increase financial stability

HARVEY McKINNON

Introduction by MAL WARWICK

DEDICATION

To Marcia, my true love and best friend.

Printed in the United States of America.

ISBN 1-56625-122-2

Library of Congress Catalog Card Number 99-60239

For more information, write or call the publisher:

    Bonus Books, Inc.

    160 E. Illinois Street

    Chicago, IL 60611

    Phone: (312) 467-0580

    e-mail: bb@bonus-books.com

    web: http://www.bonus-books.com

10   9   8   7   6   5   4   3   2   1

 printed on recycled paper

How monthly giving will build donor loyalty,
boost your organization's income,
and increase financial stability

CONTENTS

INTRODUCTION
Why you should read this book, and what you can get from it

obody knows how much money North American charities raise through monthly sustainer or pledge programs. But there are a few things we fundraisers do know from direct experience over many years:

- These programs account for a large and growing share of contributed income to nonprofit organizations with large constituencies of individual donors or members.

- Monthly giving has considerable appeal for younger donors, who are often attracted by the ease and convenience of monthly giving and by the way modest monthly contributions can become major gifts over time.

- Monthly giving has growing appeal for older donors, who tend to live on a budget and often must carefully plan their gifts to the charities they support.

- Monthly giving is a perfect example of the long-term relationship-building that growing numbers of fundraisers are apt to consider the heart of our work.

- Monthly donors are far more likely to leave bequests or consider other forms of planned gifts than are occasional or even reliable annual donors, so they're of special interest to fundraisers caught up in another pronounced trend: the veritable explosion of activity in planned giving.

If your organization does *not* operate a monthly giving program, this book will tell you everything you need to know to get one started. If your organization already has a monthly giving program, you're bound to gain new insights about a topic that most nonprofits discuss only behind closed doors.

- You'll understand why monthly giving programs are one of the fastest-growing, highest-potential techniques in fundraising today.

- You'll learn which kinds of people are most likely to join a monthly giving program and how to find them.

- You'll discover which arguments appeal most effectively to prospective monthly donors.

- You'll gain appreciation for the wide range of options open to you in designing a monthly giving program and how to choose among them.

- You'll learn how to promote loyalty and sustain giving over the long term.

- You'll find out how to coax more and bigger gifts from monthly donors.

- You'll discover how to expand a successful monthly giving program.

- You'll see scores of real-world examples drawn from successful monthly giving programs in several countries.

I feel confident making these claims because, as far as I can tell, Harvey McKinnon knows more about monthly giving programs than anyone else in the world. For more than 20 years, Harvey has specialized in this field. He has launched, managed, inspired, advised, and evaluated monthly giving programs for hundreds of nonprofit organizations in Canada, the United States, Australia, and the United Kingdom. He has amassed a collection of sample mailings from monthly giving programs that is likely the most extensive anywhere. (Sometimes I wonder how much that collection costs him every month!)

In short, Harvey McKinnon is the Master of Monthly Giving. No one else is better equipped to write the definitive book on that topic. That's exactly what you'll find between these covers.

All the best of luck to you!

— *Mal Warwick*

FOREWORD

Why I've written this book and how you'll benefit from following my advice

I have written this book to help you and your organization build a highly profitable monthly donor program. It's that simple. In the following pages, you'll discover how to obtain spectacular financial rewards and increase your organization's stability and long-term financial well-being.

Today nearly *all* fundraisers face many challenges:

- increased competition
- rising postal rates
- increasing fundraising costs
- direct mail and telemarketing programs that aren't performing as well today as in the past
- an aging donor base
- increased public scrutiny of organizations

You may even face:

- a reduction in your fundraising staff
- declining income
- more and more donors who renew only after a dozen approaches
- increasing numbers of donors who lapse forever
- a shrinking donor base
- lower average gifts

This book can help you face your increased competition and mounting fundraising costs. By applying my advice, you'll raise more money from your current donors, reduce the rate of donor attrition, and build long-term security (possibly for yourself as well as your nonprofit organization!).

Donor loyalty is central

I base my successful approach to fundraising on two interconnected techniques:

1. establishing monthly giving clubs
2. promoting donor loyalty

This two-pronged approach has helped many organizations prosper. And, if you follow the steps outlined here, you and your organization will profit, too.

In this book, you'll find repeated references to the importance of building long-term relationships with donors, though I frequently call it donor loyalty. The writer who has best given voice to this long-term perspective is my friend Ken Burnett, who developed (among many other things) a highly successful monthly giving program for Greenpeace in the United Kingdom. I strongly recommend that you read Ken's books, *Relationship Fundraising* and *Friends for Life: Relationship Fundraising in Practice*. They're among the most useful fundraising books you'll ever read.

Developing a strong relationship with your donors should be the dream of all development officers and executive directors. But many organizations neglect to cultivate lasting relationships. They favor the illusory benefits of short-term income instead. One of my goals in this book is to help you and your organization refocus on donor relationships and the Long-Term Value of your donors.

Establishing a monthly donor program is a great way to focus on the basics of service and loyalty. It's also a great way to raise much more money.

Why I feel I can help you

I believe I've helped more organizations build monthly donor programs than anyone else in North America. My video, *How to Build a Highly Profitable Monthly Giving Program*, has been used by organizations worldwide. I've written some of the first articles on monthly giving for leading publications in both the UK and the U.S. I've personally presented sessions on the subject and consulted with nonprofits in Australia, the United Kingdom, Canada, and the United States.

I've helped organizations raise many millions of dollars through monthly giving. My experience can help you save money when you start a monthly giving program and help you make more money if you already have a program in place.

How I got started

In 1976, I joined the national board of Oxfam-Canada. I was only 23, but I was enthusiastic and willing to commit 40 volunteer hours a week, in order to avoid writing my master's thesis.

Oxfam was founded in the 1940s and today it is one of the world's largest nonprofit organizations. Oxfam focused on long-term development in the Third World before long-term development was widely regarded as the best, or proper, way to spend aid dollars. It remains an organization for which I have great respect.

It was at Oxfam that I discovered monthly donor programs.

It actually took me a few years for the real value to sink in. Some genius had started a monthly donor program at Oxfam-Canada in the 1960s, but it had never been developed to its full potential. Donors initially gave by post-dated checks or through electronic funds transfer (EFT), so Oxfam was certainly one of the first charities in North America to employ EFT.

When I first joined Oxfam's staff, only five percent of our income came from monthly donors. Promotion of the program consisted of an information brochure and a "Please send more information" check-off box on reply forms.

I was hired by Oxfam-Canada in 1979. At that time, the organization had a very decentralized structure. There were three regional monthly programs going by different names: one was SharePlan, the name used today. One I forget. And the other was the donor-unfriendly World Development Tax, a name worth forgetting.

When I started work, Oxfam had seen eight years of declining income. Another fundraiser, the talented Ken Wyman, was hired around the same time and was largely responsible for reversing the income decline. Ken started promoting the SharePlan program, but the internal political climate in Oxfam at the time was decidedly unfriendly to fundraising. Both of us had to struggle for resources. (Perhaps you've experienced this as well!)

Luckily, Oxfam's attitude towards fundraising has changed over the years. Today, SharePlan has grown to contribute about 40 percent of Oxfam's income, and in a few years I believe it will reach 50 percent. Oxfam-Canada has had a monthly giving program for almost 25 years. Every year it continues to grow, both in numbers of new donors and in share of the organization's income.

But it took until 1984 for SharePlan's potential to be realized. That's the year we conducted an emergency campaign to combat a catastrophic famine in Ethiopia. SharePlan income increased dramatically. But you don't need a disaster to grow a monthly giving program! By applying the techniques you'll learn in this book, you can realize significant profits immediately.

I hope this book adds to your treasure chest of ideas, revives forgotten concepts, and stimulates your thinking about how you can build better relationships with your donors and increase their giving.

– Harvey McKinnon

A FEW WORDS OF THANKS

A thank you is important in fundraising, and also in books. All books rely on many contributors, through a sharing of ideas, various forms of support, and inspiration. This book relies on all three, and I thank the many friends and acquaintances who helped make this book possible. I especially want to thank the millions of caring donors who make monthly giving a subject of attention because of their ongoing pledges.

Many people shared their valuable experiences: Joe White, Bob Penner, and Rich Fox, all of whom recruit monthly donors through telemarketing; Dave Watson, Jim Fleckenstein, Jody Boyce, Paul Kralovanec, Mary Toropov, and Ken Malette, who shared details about their success at their nonprofits; and EFT specialists Bob Wesolowski and Willits Sawyer.

Many others contributed samples, including some excellent ones that we couldn't print because of space limitations. But whether your samples are included or not, I sincerely thank Cory Scott Whittier, Moira H. Kavanagh, Kay Lautman, Emmi Albers, Terry Murray, Steve Thomas, Tom McCabe, Brian and Sandy Loffler, Paul Karps, and Deborah Block.

Julie Weston sent me a number of samples from Asia, and Ken Burnett sent many from the UK. Both of these Brits are full of great ideas, generosity, and humor, so I thank you for your friendship and assistance. And if I missed anyone who sent me samples I apologize for neglecting to give you credit.

I greatly appreciate my co-workers Andrea Johnston, Lynn Booth, Donna Barker, Ann Gillespie, Michele Davidson, and Jeff Topham for their support and work on the book. For their comments on various sections, I'm grateful to Victor Janoff and Cathy Crouse. One of North America's finest actors, and my adorable sister-in-law, Kristen Thomson, was an immense help in editing sections and structuring this book. And thanks to my old friend Kris Klaasen who designed the book's cover.

Many clients, who are also friends, helped provide me with material: Leanne MacDonnell and May Low of BCACL, Viki Wilson of the David

Suzuki Foundation, Kathy Ward and Heather Morgan of AICR, and Mike McGee of the Sierra Legal Defence Fund.

A special thanks also to Bob Wesolowski and Carol Czuko, who were immensely helpful on the details of EFT and credit card transactions in the U.S., and to Con Squires, my friend and mentor, who taught me a lot of what I know about direct marketing.

I thank Steven Hitchcock, Ina Cooper, Mwosi Swenson, and Zoe Newman of Mal Warwick & Associates for their support. In particular, I'd like to thank Nick Allen (one of my favorite people in the world) for his work on the book, and Bobbye Dones who did a wonderful job designing the book and putting it all together in the past few months.

This book would not have happened if it weren't for the wonderful friendship and support of Mal Warwick, one of the most talented people in the business. His great editing abilities and coaching means you will get much more out of this book. Mal, thanks for everything.

Lastly, I am grateful to my wife, Marcia Thomson, and my son James, for their support, love, and inspiration.

CHAPTER 1
How monthly giving works, and why

The call for help came at 8:37 p.m. I was still in my office, writing a fundraising letter. The caller was a journalist who had no telemarketing experience, but his call was effective—I decided to give.

The year was 1979. I had just started working with Oxfam-Canada, one of Canada's largest charities.

The phone call came from one of three journalist friends, dining at a Greek restaurant across the street. At the end of their dinner, they realized they didn't have enough money to cover the bill. Apparently in 1979 a journalist couldn't get a credit card. I was their salvation, or so they thought. I crossed the street, chatted with my friends, had a cup of coffee, paid the rest of the bill . . . and used my leverage.

To repay my Good Samaritan gesture, I suggested they contribute to Oxfam. (Since there were no volunteers to do the asking, I seized the moment.) The best way to give, I said, was through Share Plan, Oxfam's monthly giving program and I just happened to have three forms already filled out with their names on them! All they had to do was decide how much they wanted to pledge each month.

One joined at $15 a month; the second pledged $25 monthly; the third, $40. Luckily, their dinner included a couple of bottles of retsina, so they readily checked off the appropriate boxes and signed their names. (Some people are willing to do anything to keep the wine and caffeine flowing!)

That was 16 years ago. Since then, Oxfam has received more than $10,000 from these three individuals, and two of the donors are still giving. The third person, my friend Doug, dropped off when he went to live in France for a year. I called him recently to see if he was still giving.

"I've been meaning to sign up again, but I just haven't taken the time to do it. Why don't you fill out a form for me, and I'll sign it?"

Doug agreed to let me tell his story in exchange for a promise: that I would not reveal that his last name is "Ward," that he writes for the *Vancouver Sun*, and that he is 45 years old.

Since my three friends are all in their forties and have proven their loyalty, Oxfam can expect many more thousands of dollars from them in the future.

The real magic in this story is that one "Ask" raised a truly major gift from middle-income donors. In fact, that initial Ask will continue to raise money every month for decades to come.

One simple Ask!

My friends have also fulfilled 100 percent of their monthly gifts, because they give automatically, through electronic funds transfer (EFT). In Canada this process is generally called "pre-authorized checking;" in Europe, "direct debit." My generous friends signed once along the dotted line. They never had to make another decision whether or not to give, only whether they should increase the amounts of their monthly gifts.

Raising more money from the same old donors

Direct mail has proven enormously successful for tens of thousands of charities in North America. Most large nonprofit donor files have been built through this method. And, along with telemarketing, direct mail is responsible for stimulating donors to give increasing amounts of money to charities every year. But it's clear that the golden days of direct mail have ended.

#219, 2211 WEST 4TH AVE.

VANCOUVER, BC

The David Suzuki Foundation

CANADA V6K 4S2

TEL: (604) 732-4228

FAX: (604) 732-0752

Jane Doe
1234 Main Street
Any City, IL 60611

Dear David,

I know environmental progress requires financial support. Here is my commitment to the Friends of the Foundation. I'll make a contribution of:

☐ **$10 monthly**   ☐ **$15 monthly**   ☐ **$20 monthly**   ☐ **$_____ monthly**

I/we authorize the David Suzuki Foundation to deduct the amount indicated above on the first day of each month from my chequing account.

Attached is a sample cheque marked VOID, to give you banking information.

I prefer to give a monthly credit card gift:

☐ VISA   ☐ MasterCard

☐ **$10 monthly**   ☐ **$15 monthly**

☐ **$20 monthly**   ☐ **$_____ monthly**

SIGNATURE _____

CARD NUMBER _____   EXPIRY DATE _____

DATE _____

SIGNATURE _____

A tax creditable receipt will be issued at the end of the year for all monthly donations made during the year.

PHONE _____

The David Suzuki Foundation

#219, 2211 WEST 4TH AVE.
VANCOUVER, BC
CANADA V6K 4S2
TEL: (604) 732-4228
FAX: (604) 732-0752

Jane Doe
1234 Main Street
Any City, IL 60611

Dear Jane

    A few years ago, you may have heard my CBC Radio series called, <u>It's a Matter of Survival</u>. I also co-authored a book with the same name.

    What I learned researching the series scared me to my very core.

    I believed then -- and believe today -- that to turn around the environmental crisis you and I have to act today.

    Just a few days ago I picked up the book I co-authored with Anita Gordon. I want to share the last paragraph with you:

    "In times of crisis, people have pulled together and forgotten their mistrust and petty rivalries. They've sacrificed and worked to change their lives. There has never been a bigger crisis than the one we now face. And we are the last generation that can pull us out of it. We must act because this is the only home we have. It is a matter of survival."

    This is the only home we have!

    Will you continue working with me to save our planet... our home? The reality is that each of us may have to sacrifice a little to save our home. We can't go on pretending everything is normal.

    You've demonstrated through your support of the Foundation that you care and that you want to stop the destruction of our environment.

    I'm writing you today because you are one of our most generous donors. And I want to invite you to join a special

"WE FIN

---

group of supporters -- the Friends of the Foundation. I'm asking if you could make a continuing commitment to the work of the David Suzuki Foundation by becoming a monthly donor.

    Could you consider becoming a Friend of the Foundation by making a donation of $15 a month to further our work?

    Your regular monthly donation will do two things: it adds up quickly to a major contribution and it allows the Foundation to make long-term plans.

    Your monthly donation could be the cost of a cup of coffee each day. But $30 a month means a significant annual tax creditable gift of $360 a year.

    But whatever amount you decide to give each month, it means an enormous difference in the work we do.

    And knowing I can count on your monthly support and that of other generous friends means we can make commitments to projects that will have a long-term impact. It truly is a matter of survival.

    So please, if you possibly can, make a decision that is an investment in the very future of our planet... our home.

    Please join with hundreds of other people who share your deep concern for the environment and become a member of the Friends of the Foundation.

    And whatever your decision, thank you for your strong support in the past -- it has done a world of good already!

Sincerely yours,

David Suzuki

P.S. The world has no shortage of environmental disasters. What it needs is environmental successes to light the way for more victories. Please join with me by becoming a Friend of the Foundation today and sending in the enclosed reply form.

An invitation package to recruit monthly donors (this page and previous) Illustration 1.1

We may even soon see a significant reduction in the volume of donor or member acquisition mailings as nonprofit organizations begin to find large-scale prospecting increasingly expensive. This is partly due to increased costs, but also because response rates to mailings continue to decline. In addition, the overwhelming majority of individuals who are ever likely to give to charities by mail or phone are already on many fundraising lists.

For most established North American nonprofits, donor lists are not growing. Many, if not most, are shrinking. Therefore, to increase income or even maintain current income levels, organizations must generate an increasing amount of money from existing donors.

Monthly giving is a perfect way to raise more money from your current donor base.

An alternative approach—taken by many charities—is simply to mail appeals more often to their donors. Take this option, however, and you're likely to burn out your donors. And then you'll have difficulty replacing them, given low prospect response rates. The alternative is to keep donors active by converting them to monthly giving. But it's crucial that you act now to set up your monthly giving program. (Your competitors may already have done so!)

For the record, here's what I mean by a *monthly giving program*. Whether it's called a "pledge program," a "sustainer program," a "monthly giving club," or something else, a monthly giving program requires that donors enter into an agreement to make regular—usually monthly—gifts to a nonprofit organization.

The organization may offer one of several mechanisms for donors to transmit their monthly gifts:

- automatic checking account transfers or "pre-authorized checking" (Electronic Funds Transfer, usually known as EFT)
- automatic credit card payments
- checks mailed in response to monthly statements
- checks mailed in pre-addressed (and sometimes dated) envelopes

Most monthly giving programs depend largely on direct mail, though telemarketing is increasingly coming into the picture (usually in combination with mail). However, some of the largest sustainer programs have been built through television advertising or space ads. And in Europe, groups have had great success with person-to-person recruiting in public places. Virtually every communications technique and channel known to the fundraising profession may be employed in a monthly giving program.

Almost any organization can develop and benefit from such a program. The size of your donor base doesn't matter. And even a new nonprofit can recruit monthly donors, so long as it has a strong case and an effective strategy to reach prospects.

Monthly giving has its limits

Be prepared: The majority of individuals on your donor file will never pledge monthly gifts to you. Don't be discouraged. If just one or two percent of your donors sign up, it will be worthwhile to develop a monthly giving program. Most organizations are able to recruit three to five percent, and I have a number of clients with more than ten percent of their donors giving monthly pledges.

Remember: The majority of your donors also neglect to include your organization in their wills, but I trust that won't stop you from launching a planned giving program.

Here are the primary reasons why people won't give on a monthly basis:

- They don't want to make commitments.
- Their jobs are insecure (or they fear that's so).
- They may be moving.
- They can't afford it.
- They're in transition—going back to school, having kids, or retiring, any of which may affect their ability to give.
- They don't believe strongly enough in your cause.
- You haven't properly asked them.
- You haven't asked often enough.
- They're elderly and don't want to make long-term commitments.
- They don't trust the technology.

These are good reasons, but don't let them stop you from starting a program.

Most philanthropically minded individuals will give to four to ten charities a year. But generally they'll only join two to four as monthly donors. (I base these observations on my Canadian experience and on research findings from Europe, where monthly giving is far better developed than in the U.S.)

When a donor joins a monthly giving club, there are consequences. She may reduce or even eliminate her gifts to other charities, because the ease of monthly giving means she doubles or triples her annual giving to the non-profit that recruited her.

Here's an example to illustrate my point:

- A donor, Cindy Williams, regularly gives a total of $1,000 a year to ten charities, or $100 each. That's her limit. Then she's successfully recruited by two of the charities into $25/month giving programs. This means she'll give those two charities a total of $600—sixty percent of her annual giving—leaving only $400 for the other eight charities. If Cindy splits the remaining money evenly, these nonprofits will see their donations decline to $50 each. This is a reduction of 50 percent.

- Cindy may even decide that she'll give $100 to four nonprofits and stop giving to four others. She could choose a combination of the above scenarios. Whatever decisions she makes, however, the clear winners are the nonprofits who invited her to join monthly giving programs. They each upgraded Cindy's annual giving by 300 percent.

- Even a nonprofit that continues to receive $100 annual donations from Cindy has lost. The organization failed to upgrade her, while two other nonprofits have dramatically increased their share of Cindy's annual giving. And she's not likely to join a third at the level of $25 a month, because her annual maximum is $1,000.

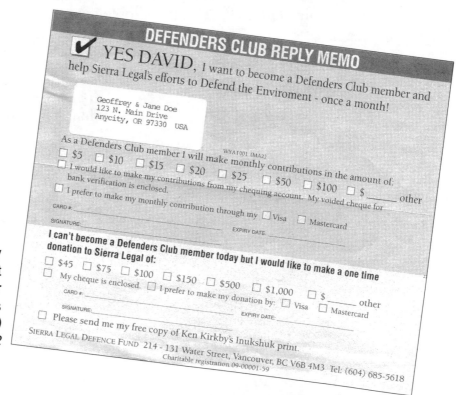

Some monthly giving recruitment packages offer single-gift options (here and page 8)
Illustration 1.2

This is why you need to approach your donors as soon as possible. Multiply the example of Cindy Williams by hundreds or thousands, and you see the potential loss to your donor income can be immense.

Equally disturbing, Cindy is far more likely to become a lapsed donor if she sends you annual gifts than if she has joined your monthly giving program. As you'll note throughout this book, I look on fundraising as a process of building relationships—and one of the biggest advantages of monthly giving is that it tends to build stronger and longer-lasting relationships with donors.

What's more, there's a good chance that Cindy didn't even select her two favorite charities when she joined those two monthly giving programs. More likely, she responded to the two charities who asked her first. Donors have told me they often have joined organizations that aren't at the top of their lists of priorities, but they continue to give because they have "made a commitment." And the successful organizations gain a greater "share" of a donor's annual giving.

An example of what can happen to annual giving when a donor joins a monthly program

Charity	Before	After Scenario 1	After Scenario 2
A	$100	$300 ($25/mo.)	$300 ($25/mo.)
B	$100	$300 ($25/mo.)	$300 ($25/mo.)
C	$100	$50	$100
D	$100	$50	$100
E	$100	$50	$100
F	$100	$50	$100
G	$100	$50	$0
H	$100	$50	$0
I	$100	$50	$0
J	$100	$50	$0
Total Annual Giving	**$1,000**	**$1,000**	**$1,000**

Like you, I believe that Sierra Legal can continue to make real headway through the use of the courts to defend our environment.

Yet, I'm frightened by what may take place in the future. Too often our work is spent slowing down the destruction. The task of stemming the destruction, and turning things around, is not going to be easy. Environmental groups across Canada will have to rise to the challenge to ensure that our natural environment is vigorously defended.

The Sierra Legal Defence Fund is committed to be there to assist the environmental community in a court of law.

But Sierra Legal will have to prepare for that challenge. And to do this we need more committed supporters to take a hands-on approach.

That's why I want to encourage you to become a member of Sierra Legal's Defenders Club.

The Defenders Club is critical to Sierra Legal's long term plans because it is our single most important means of support on a month to month basis.

Defenders Club members make monthly automatic donations from their chequing account

DEFENCE FUND

Geoffrey & Jane Doe
123 N. Main Drive
Anycity, OR 97330 USA

Dear Geoffrey and Jane,

I'm writing to ask you to join something very important for the protection of our environment.

You have generously demonstrated your support for the Sierra Legal Defence Fund by making financial contributions in the past. This support has allowed Sierra Legal to become one of the most effective environmental organizations in Canada. Effective because we use a very powerful tool to defend our environment -- the law.

Your past support has been critical to our success and for this I would like to thank you very much. I want to invite you now to become part of Sierra Legal's most important program.

I would like to ask if you would be willing to make an on-going commitment by joining Sierra Legal's Defenders Club of monthly donors.

over please

A special invitation to join a monthly donor club.
Illustration 1.2

CHAPTER 2
Seven great reasons to start your monthly giving program—right now

There are at least seven great reasons for you to rush out right away and start a monthly giving program for your organization:

1.   You'll dramatically increase your annual income.

In studies I've conducted, donors have generally given at least 100 percent more money once they sign up for a monthly giving program.

In many cases, their annual giving is dramatically higher, up to 1200 percent higher.

Typically, a donor who contributes two $25 gifts per year, for a total of $50, will sign up for monthly giving at $10 or more per month. That's at least $120 per year, or nearly two-and-a-half times the donor's previous total annual giving. In seven years, your $10-a-month donor will give you $840.

The majority of monthly gifts range between $10 and $20 for most organizations. (Your average monthly contribution will depend on how big your entry-level gift is, how long your program has been up and running, how aggressively you seek to increase monthly gifts, how successful other parts of your program are, how good your copy is, and other factors.)

2.   You build a better relationship with your donors.

Monthly giving programs can help draw donors closer to your organization. They become among the best people to approach for special events, and they're the people most likely to leave your organization money in their wills.

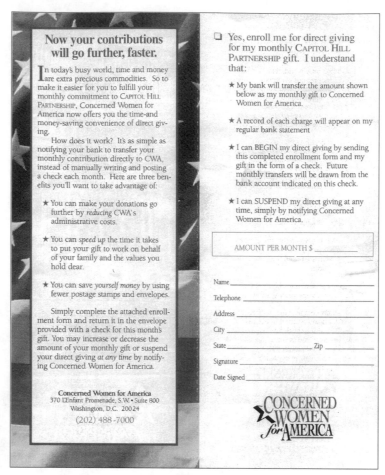

A brochure
promoting
monthly giving
Illustration 2.1

3. Donors will stay with your organization longer.

In long-term value studies, I've learned that monthly donors are going to be with you for 5-10 years—especially if they give via Electronic Funds Transfer (EFT). Many will give until they die.

4. Monthly giving revenue is predictable.

You are guaranteed a minimum level of income every month. This money will cover monthly overhead costs and help cash flow. This can be especially helpful for smaller nonprofits.

5. You'll lower your fundraising costs.

You don't have to (and should not) send monthly donors all your direct mail appeals. Every organization we've worked with has lowered its administrative costs and increased its income through monthly giving programs.

Your monthly donors will be one of the most profitable segments of your donor base, especially if you use EFT, which is very inexpensive to maintain. One of our clients has just one staff person who manages a program of 6,500 monthly EFT donors, who give $2 million a year. (Of course, nonprofits that mail monthly reminders have much higher administrative costs.)

Income for 50 New Monthly Donors - $12.36 Entry Level

year	# in progress	% fulfillment	average gift	max. # gifts	est. # gifts	year income	cum. $	cost / memb.	cost / year	cum. cost	profit	cum. profit
1	50	80%	$12.36	600	480	$5,933	$5,933	$20	$1,000	$1,000	$4,933	$4,933
2	40	80%	14.00	480	384	5,376	11,309	15	600	1,600	4,776	9,709
3	32	80%	15.00	384	307	4,608	15,917	16	512	2,112	4,096	13,805
4	29	90%	16.00	346	311	4,977	20,893	17	490	2,602	4,487	18,292
5	26	90%	17.00	311	280	4,759	25,652	18	467	3,068	4,292	22,584
6	23	90%	18.00	280	252	4,535	30,187	19	443	3,511	4,092	26,676
7	21	90%	20.00	252	227	4,535	34,722	20	420	3,931	4,115	30,791
8	19	90%	22.00	227	204	4,490	39,212	21	397	4,328	4,093	34,884
9	17	90%	24.00	204	184	4,408	43,620	22	374	4,702	4,034	38,918
10	15	90%	25.00	184	165	4,132	47,752	23	352	5,054	3,780	42,698

1. The fulfillment rate is an average of EFT, credit card, and monthly statements.

2. The $12.36 is a general average for monthly giving programs.

3. The percentage fulfillment will go up because:

   a) donors who stay are more loyal

   b) donors are more likely to be in EFT/credit card streams, and

   c) you'll convert monthly reminder people to EFT and credit cards over the years, thus increasing their fulfillment rate.

4. The income does not stop in Year 10, but continues to grow and should eventually double the 10-year giving amount before all donors stop giving.

5. This is a chart for the ten-year giving history of donors who enter in one particular year. The program will have new people entering on a regular basis. This chart shows how valuable new donors are.

6. The average income from each new donor at the $12.36 entry level over just a ten-year period, taking into consideration drop-off rates and upgrades, will be $853.96.

This table shows the value of 50 monthly donors over a ten-year period and demonstrates how valuable these donors are to you

6. **Your income will continue to grow over time.**

   A $15 monthly donor gives $180 a year, or $1,260 over a seven-year period. But upgrading can increase that amount. For example, in a recent mailing for one of our clients, 33 percent of the donors on the file increased their gifts by an average of $5 per month, or $60 a year. That's $60 a year extra for every upgrading donor!

7. **Monthly giving is convenient.**

   It's easy for you, and it's easy for the donor.

Income for 500 New Monthly Donors - $24 Entry Level

year	# in program	% fulfillment	average gift	max. # gifts	est. # gifts	year income	cum. $	cost / memb.	cost / year	cum. cost	profit	cum. profit
1	500	90%	$24.00	6,000	5,400	$129,600	$129,600	$20	$10,000	$10,000	$119,600	$119,600
2	450	90%	25.00	5,400	4,860	121,500	251,500	15	6,750	16,750	114,750	234,350
3	405	90%	26.00	4,860	4,374	113,274	364,824	16	6,480	23,230	107,244	341,594
4	365	90%	27.00	4,374	3,937	106,288	471,112	17	6,197	29,427	100,092	441,686
5	328	90%	28.00	3,937	3,543	99,202	570,315	18	5,905	35,331	93,297	534,983
6	295	90%	30.00	3,543	3,189	95,659	665,974	19	5,610	40,941	90,050	625,033
7	266	90%	31.00	3,189	2,870	88,963	754,937	20	5,314	46,255	83,649	708,682
8	239	90%	33.00	2,870	2,583	85,233	840,170	21	5,022	51,278	80,210	788,892
9	215	90%	35.00	2,583	2,325	81,358	921,528	22	4,735	56,013	76,623	865,515
10	194	90%	36.00	2,325	2,092	75,315	996,842	23	4,455	60,468	70,859	936,374

1. The 90% fulfillment is the minimum you should receive using EFT and credit cards.

2. The $24 is not an unrealistic figure for the UWSB, given the workplace averages.

3. The income does not stop in Year 10, but continues to grow and should eventually double the 10-year giving amount before all donors stop giving.

4. This is a chart for the ten-year giving history of donors who enter on one particular year. The program will have new people entering on a regular basis. This chart shows how valuable new donors are.

5. This average income for each new donor at the $24 entry level over just a ten-year period, taking into consideration drop-off rates and upgrades, will be $1,993.68.

A look at the value of 500 EFT and credit card donors
at a high average monthly gift level

CHAPTER 3

Your monthly giving choices, and how to make them

Your donors are already on a monthly cycle. (Yes, even the males.) Many people receive monthly paychecks. And nearly everyone receives a phone bill, a credit card bill, an electricity bill, and perhaps bills for their mortgage, cable, insurance, and the like—every month.

Because people are used to paying monthly invoices, the majority of us organize our financial management around a monthly schedule. So it's logical for us to consider supporting the causes we believe in on a monthly basis.

Who are your potential monthly donors?

I believe 3 to 5 percent of the individuals on any donor file will join a monthly program. I have clients with 11 percent, 14 percent, and 24 percent of their donors participating in such programs. A strong monthly giving program tends to grow over time, as new monthly givers are recruited and the old ones stay loyal.

In many European nonprofit organizations, more than 50 percent of the donors give monthly. Some of these groups no longer even ask for single gifts!

In North America, child sponsorship programs are based on monthly pledges. This accounts for a majority of their donors—and 90 to 95 percent of their income.

There is nothing magical about knowing who will make a monthly commitment. You'll find individuals on monthly giving files who are old, young, or middle-aged—people of all races, both male and female, all religions, and all political persuasions.

In most organizations, there are more women than men enrolled in monthly giving programs—60 percent of the monthly givers, at times.

 **VanCity**

Vancouver City Savings Credit Union

ALL IN ONE STATEMENT

WEST 4TH AVENUE COMMUNITY BRANCH

2233 4TH AVENUE WEST
VANCOUVER BC V6K 1N9
877 7000
B.C. TOLL FREE 1-800-980-8777

HARVEY MCKINNON
1234 WEST AVENUE #4
VANCOUVER BC V4K 1N2

Your
Personal
Financial
Record

DATE 27 APRIL
ACCOUNT: 002938
BRANCH: 1

DATE	TRANSACTION DETAIL	AMOUNT	BALANCE
	IMPORTANT: UNDER YOUR AGREEMENT WITH VANCITY, THIS STATEMENT WILL BE CONSIDERED CORRECT IF NO EXCEPTIONS ARE REPORTED IN WRITING WITHIN 30 DAYS FROM MAILING TO YOU. RATES QUOTED AS AT STATEMENT DATE. GST NO. R105483150		
	CHEQUING SAVINGS		
#1	CREDITLINE		
	BALANCE FROM PREVIOUS STATEMENT		2,318.08
28 MAR 98	CHEQUE # 157	70.00	2,248.08
31 MAR 98	CHEQUE # 161	65.00	2,183.08
31 MAR 98	CHEQUE # 153	20.00	2,163.08
01 APR 98	PREAUTHORIZED PYMT TO BC ASSOC COM LIVING	20.00	2,143.08
01 APR 98	PREAUTHORIZED PYMT TO OXFAM-CANADA	35.00	2,108.08
02 APR 98	ATM CASH WITHDRAWAL 2233 W 4TH AVE VANCOUVER BC	200.00	1,908.08
02 APR 98	TRANSFER TO CHEQUING SAVINGS # 1 (ACCT 289850)	793.00	1,115.08
02 APR 98	CHEQUE # 103	440.00	675.08
03 APR 98	TRANSFER TO CHEQUING SAVINGS # 1 (ACCT 289850)	200.00	475.08
03 APR 98	CHEQUE # 156	28.50	446.58
06 APR 98	DEPOSIT	1,536.83	1,983.41
06 APR 98	CHEQUE # 159	70.00	1,913.41
07 APR 98	ATM CASH WITHDRAWAL 2233 W 4TH AVE VANCOUVER BC	200.00	1,713.41
10 APR 98	TRANSFER TO LOAN # 4	1,094.57	618.84
14 APR 98	ATM CASH WITHDRAWAL 2233 W 4TH AVE VANCOUVER BC	200.00	418.84
15 APR 98	PREAUTHORIZED PYMT TO ETHICAL FUNDS INC.	200.00	218.84
15 APR 98	CHEQUE DEPOSIT	1,536.83	1,755.67
16 APR 98	TRANSFER TO CHEQUING SAVINGS # 1 (ACCT 289850)	793.00	962.67
17 APR 98	TRANSFER TO CHEQUING SAVINGS # 1 (ACCT 289850)	200.00	762.67
20 APR 98	ATM CASH WITHDRAWAL 2233 W 4TH AVE VANCOUVER BC	200.00	562.67
20 APR 98	CHEQUE # 155	70.00	492.67
27 APR 98	ATM CASH WITHDRAWAL 2233 W 4TH AVE VANCOUVER BC	200.00	292.67
27 APR 98	ACCOUNT SERVICE CHARGE	9.50	283.17

LINE OF CREDIT	$5,000.00	CURRENT RATE	9.500%		
	CURRENT DUE	$0.00	TOTAL CREDITS	3,073.66	
	PAST DUE	$0.00	TOTAL DEBITS	5,108.57	
	TOTAL DUE	$0.00	7 CHEQUES		

U.S. $ SAVINGS

#1	US DOLLAR SAVINGS		
	BALANCE FROM PREVIOUS STATEMENT		1.72

CONTINUE ON REVERSE

PRINTED ON RECYCLED PAPER

Bank statement with pre-authorized EFT
Illustration 3.1

Weighing the options

There are three primary ways to collect monthly pledges for your organization: monthly invoices, credit cards, and Electronic Funds Transfer (EFT). Let's look at each of these in turn.

Monthly invoices. You can mail a monthly invoice or statement, which donors are to return with a check each month.

Credit cards. You can receive pledges through credit card debits on a regular basis. Credit cards offer convenience and a grace period before payment is due—and everyone's familiar with them. (Donors may even receive frequent flyer points!) Anything that makes giving easier for donors should make you more money. As well, a number of charities I've worked with have found that credit card gifts tend to be higher on the average than those fulfilled via either EFT or paper checks. But this varies from organization to organization.

Electronic Funds Transfer. By mutual agreement, you can arrange for a donor's gift to be transferred automatically from her bank account to your organization's. EFT entails no envelopes and no reminders. A donor's monthly bank statement includes either a form that states the amount transferred, or a listing incorporated into the statement itself.

To establish an EFT, the donor needs only fill out a simple form authorizing the monthly transfer of money to your organization, include a sample check marked "Void," and sign the form. (Some groups take "live" signed checks, copy the necessary bank coding, then deposit them to fulfill the first gift. I've seen some problems with this arrangement, because some people only want to make a one-time gift and accidentally indicate they'll pay monthly. However, in the U.S. about 80 percent of the first monthly gifts come from a live check and you get to start a person faster this way. You should always keep monthly donor authorization forms in case a problem arises. And it will. Some people will join and forget they've done so.)

Nonprofits that have had monthly giving programs for several decades used to "bill" donors by sending out reminder notices with reply envelopes. Volunteers dutifully stuffed envelopes and recorded gift information. The intentions were good. Money was raised. But it was an inefficient system and, consequently, it often fell short of expectations. Though some organizations still generate monthly billing statements manually, computerization has made the practice far more effective.

In recent years, most organizations have employed computerized billing systems that allow them to include "personal notes" to their donors. These personal notes usually consist of 30 words or less and refer to a donor's status (e.g., notifying her she missed the previous month's payment).

The vast majority of monthly donors in Canada, Europe, and Australia now give by electronic means, primarily via EFT. By contrast, the majority of monthly gifts in the United States still come from individuals who receive monthly reminder statements by mail, and then send their checks.

Friends for Life Membership Acceptance Form

FROM
    Jana Doe
    345 4th Street
    First City, CA 99002

                  AE5FL1   00066324922

Dear Marilyn,

Yes, I accept your invitation to become a **Charter Member** of **Friends for Life**. I understand the need for a dependable source of funds to **fight cancer**. I'm willing to donate the following amount **each month**:

☐ $5 ☐ $10 ☐ $15 ☐ $25 ☐ $ _____ Other

I prefer to donate by one of the following

1 ■ **Credit Card**

☐ VISA ☐ MasterCard Credit card no. _____

SIGNATURE _____   EXPIRATION _____

2 ■ **Automatic bank transfer***

☐ I authorize AICR to receive the above amount from my checking account on the first day of each month.

SIGNATURE _____   DATE _____

☐ I have enclosed a check marked VOID, for bank coding purposes.

3 ■ **Monthly Check**

☐ I understand I'll receive a monthly statement.

YOUR GUARANTEE: You may cancel your gift at any time. You'll receive member benefits in recognition of your contributions, including a mug for $15 or more.

However you decide to join, please provide your phone number for verification: _____

☐ Please send me more information on Friends for Life.
☐ I prefer to give a single gift of $ _____

You can call Eve toll-free **1-800-843-8114** and join today. She'll be happy to help you.

American Institute for Cancer Research, 1759 R. Street, NW, Washington, DC 20069-2012

* Please Note: When you give by credit card or bank transfer you save writing a monthly check. And you reduce AICR's mail costs. This means more of your gift goes to fighting cancer.

Membership acceptance form
Illustration 3.2

Most monthly donors are recruited through direct mail and telemarketing, although there are notable exceptions, with leads generated through space advertising and television. In any case, monthly donors who receive regular invoices must be highly responsive to direct mail. After all, you expect twelve mail-generated gifts each year! Even if you've acquired these monthly donors through a personal solicitation or a phone call, they'll still have to respond by mail each month to fulfill their pledges. For those individuals who aren't strongly mail-responsive, the attrition rate will be higher.

The donors you recruit through non-direct mail means, and who give by credit card or EFT, may be less responsive to direct mail. But their fulfillment rates will be higher, and they'll give for longer periods of time. So, when you recruit donors, through any method, a *special emphasis should be put on getting them to give by electronic means.*

In Canada, Australia, and Europe, many charities don't offer monthly billing statements as a giving option. Instead, they give donors two choices —credit cards or EFT—and sometimes only one: EFT. Particularly in the U.S., such a policy is likely to attract fewer donors to a monthly giving program. However, even in the United States, this may make sense for some organizations.

For one thing, by not offering a billing option, the charity may lower administrative and fundraising costs—and not significantly affect net income. You'll have to make an assessment of which options you choose for your organization. Your decision will be based on many factors, including:

- average gift size
- who you'll ask to join
- your staff resources

Other monthly giving options

Less frequently used methods of collecting monthly gifts include post-dated checks, monthly envelopes, and payroll deduction.

Post-dated checks. Even though they are apparently illegal in some American states, I was once enrolled in a monthly giving program in which I gave a small U.S. nonprofit organization twelve post-dated checks each year. Neither party to this transaction was sent to jail. Post-dated checks are legal in Canada and many other countries.

For small nonprofits this is an option worth considering. Fulfillment is near 100 percent, just like credit cards and EFT. And you save the high cost of having to mail your donors a special invoice each month, and having to rely on them to respond.

Like electronic giving, if a donor wants to stop the checks from being deposited, she must initiate contact with you. (Inertia is the fundraiser's friend when you have post-dated checks or a commitment through EFT or credit cards!)

The obvious drawback of post-dated checks is you have to renew a commitment and collect a new series of checks from a donor. You want to start asking for a new series of checks before you've deposited an individual's last check. And you do this through a series of reminders, probably first by mail, since it's more cost-effective. (A follow-up phone call may be the next step.)

The staff or volunteers at some small nonprofits can personally recruit supporters to write post-dated checks. You can also solicit post-dated checks for specific projects with specific time limits.

Monthly envelopes. Monthly reply envelopes are a variation on monthly billing statements especially suited for low-dollar monthly donors. You can send them twelve envelopes stamped January, February, March, etc.—either all at once, or in three or four batches in the course of the year. They could be wallet-flap envelopes with attached reply forms, or plain envelopes with small detached reply forms. You could even give them stickers to place on their calendars ("Greenpeace Gift" or "Orphan's Fund"). This will remind those of us with bad memories to send in our checks.

The sample on the next page from TreePeople is a hefty package that includes an 8-1/2" x 11" letter, twelve reply forms, and twelve envelopes. The reply envelopes have the month stamped on the front. Each stamp looks different, to give the impression that they could have been hand-stamped, a personal touch. They use a red stamp for the month, and the other type on the envelope is green. (Note: TreePeople uses this approach with $15-per-month donors.)

If you send envelopes, I recommend you test sending them to your donors on a quarterly basis, three envelopes at a time. This will save on monthly mailing costs and staff time. It may also help people avoid losing their envelopes. And it may result in a higher profit.

If you send the envelopes in batches of three, and your organization is, for example, an inner-city mission, teaser copy on the reply envelopes could read:

- April: Food
- May: Clothing
- June: Shelter

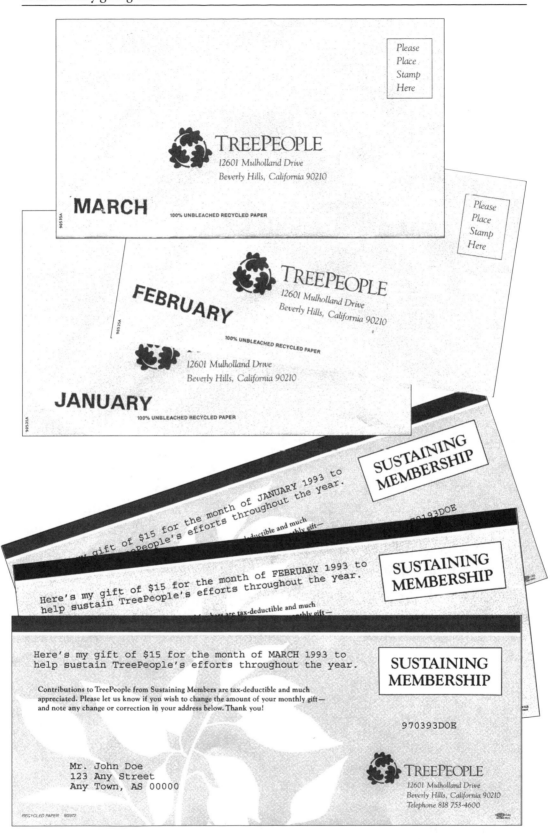

This charity sends twelve reply forms and twelve envelopes
in a large package to their donors each year
Illustration 3.3

Or, if you worked for an international aid agency:
- July: Water Projects
- August: Refugees
- September: Seeds and Tools

An environmental group could use them with copy such as:
- October: Forest Preservation
- November: Clean Water
- December: Reindeers, Not Cars

If you use this system, the advantages of quarterly envelopes will be:
- You get to make your case on a regular basis, as opposed to once a year.
- There is less likelihood that a donor will lose her envelopes and stop fulfilling.
- You are more likely to be able to track down a donor shortly after a move and therefore maintain her giving.

When you've sent 12 envelopes and discover that a donor hasn't given for two months, you must take action immediately. Assume he's lost the envelopes, and send him a letter (and new envelopes). Mention in your letter that you've noticed he hasn't sent checks for two months, and you thought it could be because he'd misplaced the envelopes. Then if you don't hear from him within four weeks, call him to find out what is going on.

As a rule, I do *not* advocate using monthly envelopes as described here. But it may be worthwhile using them with extremely low-dollar donors. For example, a donor who has pledged $3 a month and fulfills each month is worth $36 a year. Mailing to her each month may be barely a break-even proposition when you take back-end costs into account. But four letters a year, each containing three envelopes, will cut down on your administrative expenses, and could increase your net profit.

Payroll deduction. Primarily used by the United Way and similar coalitions of nonprofit agencies, this form of regular giving is highly lucrative. Deductions are made either on a semi-weekly or monthly basis depending on pay schedules and the donor's choice. Regardless of the payment schedule, these are committed donors and very generous ones. Payroll deduction is similar to EFT, but slightly less effective, since the recipient nonprofit usually loses a donor when she leaves a company.

Many United Way affiliates receive substantial funds from the employees of larger corporations or government offices, often averaging $200-$300 a year. Deducting $25 from a monthly paycheck is easy for the donor and convenient for the agency—and it dramatically increases the amount an individual will give. But given continuing layoffs by larger corporations and government agencies, many people will be moving to work in smaller companies or setting up their own businesses. Thus, United Way canvassers are less likely to reach them in their new offices. Converting payroll donors to EFT is a way to maintain giving, since most people will continue giving even after they transfer jobs (so long as they haven't moved to a new community represented by a different United Way).

This response device offers donors
three ways to send monthly gifts
Illustration 3.4

In many communities, the United Way allows designated gifts to non-United Way charities. That way, your organization may be able to receive monthly gifts through the United Way. And many United Ways will transfer gifts, including monthly pledges, to your organization with no charge. (There is usually a United Way restriction that a non-member organization receiving gifts must be a registered charitable organization.) The United Ways that allow donor-designated gift programs are numerous, but you'll have to check the policy in your area to see if this is an option for you.

There are also other federations of charities that are growing rapidly and focusing on payroll collection, so the same potential for monthly giving exists through these as well.

CHAPTER 4
Challenging the misconceptions about monthly giving

For some reason, many fundraisers have proven to be creative in the many ways they object to starting monthly giving programs. Here are seven of the most common objections:

1. "It won't work with our donor base."

A few years ago a large European charity spent a fortune mailing to their entire list an invitation package with what (in hindsight) was obviously the wrong monthly giving proposition. The details don't matter: They may have asked for too much money, or too little. They may have made the offer look complicated. Or perhaps they didn't spell out the benefits to the donor. Whatever the explanation, the offer bombed. And the people in charge of fundraising in that organization concluded that their donors wouldn't go for a monthly giving program. Just two years later, however, after developing the proper proposition, they now make more than 60 percent of their income from monthly donors—and it grows every month.

2. "Our donors are too old."

I have a large U.S. nonprofit client, 30 percent of whose donors are 65 or older. Some 29 percent of their monthly donors are 65 or over—the same proportion. I have other clients with seniors as monthly donors in *greater* proportions than their numbers. Take it from me, seniors are just as likely to pledge as younger people.

3. "Our donors aren't committed enough."

In my experience, *any* nonprofit organization can make a significant amount of money from a monthly giving program. (Anyway, you don't know until you try it!)

4. "It's a small amount of money."

Guess again! I worked with a medium-sized Australian nonprofit that started a monthly giving program from scratch. Over 11 years, the program grew from nothing to 11,512 monthly donors generating annual income of $3,492,381. This is in a country of 20 million people. And the program is still growing rapidly.

Foster Parents Plan of Canada, which is based on monthly donors, raises close to $34,000,000 annually in a country of 30 million.

The success of your program will be based on many factors: the product, the offer, the benefits to the donor, the media you use, your budget, and the copy or pitch.

5. "It's too much work."

Monthly giving programs can easily be streamlined. For example, you could contract out the EFT and credit card processing to a service bureau. To reduce staff time and costs, you could decide not to offer a check option. You could hire a consultant to develop the strategy and deliver the creative work. A monthly giving club may be the most cost-effective element in your development program.

6. "We tested it, and it didn't work."

This is by far the most irritating misconception about monthly giving.

I remember a decade ago at a Direct Marketing Association meeting, the manager of one of Canada's largest nonprofits stood up and said, "Personalization doesn't work. We tried it." I thought he was one candle short of a chandelier, and under questioning he revealed the details of his so-called personalization test. He had simply addressed donors as *Dear Mrs. Hamburger* or *Dear Mr. Frankfurter* instead of *Dear Friend*. Obviously, he was unaware that effective personalization involves far more than simply inserting a donor's name here and there: It requires using information *about* the donor that will lend a unique, personal touch to the letter. Yet he was willing to pontificate publicly about his "test." Worse, he abandoned his donor base to *Dear Friend* letters for who knows how long.

I tell this story because it's far too common for nonprofit managers to base their decisions on faulty research. If you're going to test, make sure you know what you're doing!

7. "We don't know how to do it."

Read this book, and re-read #6.

Your program will work if well done, and it will bomb if you do it badly.

Contributor Reply Memo

Oxfam CANADA

TO: David Gallagher
Oxfam-Canada

FROM: Mr. Harvey Seed
1636 Maple St.
Vancouver, B.C.
V6J 3S4

24499
1052123

Here's my year-end donation to help people build peace
and self-reliance.

MY SINGLE DONATION

( ) I am able to renew my commitment to Oxfam at this
time. Enclosed is a gift of $35.00.

OR ( ) I can even give:
( ) $25.00 ( ) $50.00 ( ) $_____

( ) I am enclosing $80.00 or more, or joining Shareplan
(see below). Please send me a free "New
Internationalist" subscription.

( ) I am giving by cheque ( ) Visa ( ) MasterCard:

Expiry Date: _____

Card no: _____ Date: _____

Signature: _____

MY MONTHLY SHAREPLAN DONATION*

( ) I'm a past Oxfam contributor. Now I'm willing to
make a monthly commitment. I'm pleased to be
able to support Oxfam's life-saving work every
month.

I will give a monthly gift of:
( ) $10.00 monthly
( ) $15.00 monthly
( ) $20.00 monthly ... only $0.66 per day
OR ( ) $_____ monthly

( ) I authorize Oxfam-Canada to withdraw the amount
indicated from my bank account or credit card.
I have enclosed a cheque marked "Void" for bank
transfers.

For Shareplan contribution by credit card please charge
to ( ) Visa ( ) MasterCard:

Expiry Date: _____

Card no: _____ Date: _____

Signature: _____

* I understand that I can change or cancel my
contribution at any time. Our charitable registration
number is 022135-03-10. Call toll-free 1-800-387-4760.

175 Carlton Street
Toronto, Ontario
M5A 4M7

(17)

Response device used with a year-end
appeal, offering monthly giving options
Illustration 4.1

So, now let me assume I've convinced you: A monthly giving
program would likely be very lucrative for your organization. But starting
a monthly giving program just doesn't seem practical to you. Let's look
at some of the most common obstacles my clients have *really* faced.

Four obstacles to starting a monthly giving program, and how to overcome them

Obstacle #1:

I don't have the financial resources to launch a monthly giving program . . .

Solutions:

- Start small! If you can't afford to develop a logo, letterhead, and special newsletter for a monthly giving program and provide valuable benefits to members, then just ask people to join a monthly program, anyway.

- Explain the convenience and cost-savings of monthly giving in your newsletter to donors or members.

- In your appeals to donors, offer monthly giving as a special way to help. Include a box on the reply form for more information (or even a section people can fill out to join immediately). Reinforce this option with a paragraph in your letter.

- Consider using volunteers to recruit members.

  Many donors will join a monthly giving program simply because you invite them to do so. One of my clients with a large donor base placed a small, 120-word promotional ad in its newsletter—and attracted 227 new monthly givers. The cost: almost nothing.

Obstacle #2:

I don't have the authority to set up a monthly giving program so I have to convince my superiors . . .

Solutions:

- Take the charts, graphs, and insights in this book, and adapt them into a presentation for the decision-makers in your organization. Try starting your proposal with the following lead sentence: "Would you prefer that our donors give once or twice a year, or every month?"

- Propose survey research (with questions on monthly giving included in any donor survey you conduct).

- Propose a test. Select the segments of your donor file most likely to become monthly givers, and test an appeal to them. Analyze the Long-Term Value of the donors who enter the program, and determine if it's worthwhile to proceed.

Obstacle #3:

I'm afraid a monthly giving program will take "too much staff time"...

Solution:

Jim Fleckenstein of the Navy Memorial Foundation (Washington, D.C.) told me that when he started his monthly giving program, he was the only staff member responsible for development. He felt that he didn't have the time or resources to run a manual monthly billing program, so he decided he would only offer EFT to his donors. His supporters tend to be conservative older males, many of whom don't even have credit cards. Yet he managed in a short period to recruit many members from his donor base with only low-intensity efforts. This has significantly increased income from these donors.

Obstacle #4:

Other staff members in our development department think a monthly giving club will "take money" from their programs...

Solutions:

Smaller nonprofits often have only one or two staff persons in the development department. Therefore, there is usually little concern about where money comes from—the concern is usually how to raise more money.

In larger organizations, there may be competition for donors and income, especially if specialized staff have particular targets to reach. Not surprisingly, a monthly giving program *will* reduce income from other areas of fundraising, principally direct mail, telemarketing, and special programs for "mid-level" donors ($50-500 annually). So, even though *overall* the nonprofit's income will increase, the new program may be threatening to staff members responsible for particular areas of the budget. (A similar situation could arise if you introduce a new telemarketing program and you pull donors from direct mail, or a major donor program that pulls the best donors out of the mail program.)

There are two ways to solve this problem: either (a) unwavering support from the decision-makers in your organization, or (b) setting up a win-win situation, with such devices as overall departmental income targets rather than targets for individual managers.

British Columbians for Mentally Handicapped People (BCMHP)'s new name is
**B.C. Association
for Community Living (BCACL)**
30 East 6th Avenue,
Vancouver, B.C. V5T 4P4
Phone (604) 875-1119

Dear Friend,

Like all new students, Liisa wondered what her first day at school would be like.

Would the other students like her?

Could she do the work?

Would the teachers be nice?

Liisa is like most students. But she is different in two ways. One, she has many challenging handicaps.

And two, she was entering a Grade 11 class and couldn't read, write or talk.

Liisa spent the first thirteen years of her life on her back in an institution.

The government said she was "too disabled to live in the community". They said she must be institutionalized for her entire life.

They were wrong.

BCACL provided legal assistance to help free her from the institution. And later, at her parents' request, helped pressure the Maple Ridge school board to allow her to enter Grade 11. The results have been amazing!

Her story is a truly inspiring tale of human courage and endurance.

In this envelope you'll find a picture of Liisa. I'm sending it to you because of what it tells us about the human spirit.

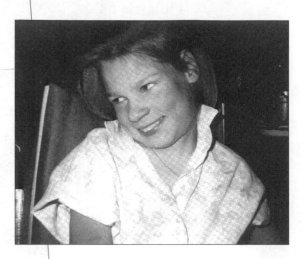

I have a copy of this photograph on my wall. More than anything else, it symbolizes to me one basic principle. Every child, regardless of disability, deserves a chance.

And, when given a chance, the child will thrive.

I saw Liisa when she was a prisoner in the institution. Her eyes were haunted, scared and anxious. I couldn't get them out of my mind.

I'd like you to look at her eyes now. They are full of

over please

...dom. She's now living with a ...doing well in school.

...ends. Friends that will be with her ...he has hopes for the future.

...n her school that differences ...are small. All of us have the same ...friendship, respect, love and happiness.

Liisa gave this precious gift of understanding to many people.

Liisa can never regain her 13 wasted years, but let's make sure this tragedy never happens again to another human being.

Today, hundreds of people with mental handicaps are being released from B.C. institutions. They and their families need your help.

Will you send a donation to help more people like Liisa? Will you return your gift to me in the enclosed envelope? Whether you can afford $25, or a gift of any amount, I need to hear from you as soon as possible. And please consider joining Pledge Partners, our monthly supporter club.

Your gift will help children and adults like Liisa realize their dreams. Please send your generous contribution today.

Yours sincerely,

Al Etmanski

Al Etmanski
Past Executive Director
BCMHP/BCACL

P.S.   Thank you for reading this letter and please don't set it aside. Many people with mental handicaps have too much at stake. Please let me hear from you today.

Liisa's eyes were once scared and haunted. Now they are full of joy and happiness!

Your support of BCMHP will help other people like Liisa realize their dreams.

Al

**This letter recruited many
monthly donors**
Illustration 4.2

CHAPTER 5
The six essential ingredients of a successful monthly giving program

I have developed successful monthly giving programs in Canada, the United States, and Australia for charities working in the areas of international aid, health care, social service and welfare, religion, peace, social justice, women's issues, advocacy, the environment, and politics. All of these groups have benefited from increased revenue from their monthly donors. Most have tripled participating donors' previous annual giving levels.

All these successful monthly giving programs are based on the premise that a nonprofit organization's most valuable asset is the loyalty of its donors—and the recognition that loyalty is a two-way street.

1. **Your organization must recognize that donor loyalty is a two-way street.**

   How well does your organization treat its donors?

   After a person's initial gift, what's your next communication? Is it a warm thank-you—or a request to give again? Not appreciation for the gift, just "Send more money, we have needs"?

   Now ask yourself, How do you personally respond when you've done someone a favor, and, instead of thanks, all you get in return is a plea for more help? If you're like me—or the vast majority of other humans on this planet—you probably feel at least a little resentful.

   Clearly, then, it should be no surprise to learn (as research confirms again and again) that donors feel mistreated when they're treated this way. Yet the number of seemingly successful nonprofits who have alienated donors by not showing proper appreciation is shocking.

   In the days when nearly every charity treated its donors equally badly, donors often endured such disdainful behavior unquestioningly. But today, when a competing charity just might send a graceful

THE ● WGBH
sustainer

February 3, 1998

Mr. John Q. Doe
1234 West Elm Street
Major City, USA 00000

Dear Mr. Doe

I would like to extend a warm welcome to you as a founding member of the WGBH Sustaining Member program. Your monthly gift of $15.00 is very much appreciated.

Your decision to provide WGBH with a reliable source of ongoing support at the Sustaining Member level is of immense value to the station. As WGBH charts new waters, Sustaining Members play a special role in helping us continue a proud tradition of creating insightful television and radio broadcasts and educational initiatives.

People often ask me how WGBH became an accomplished producer of award-winning programs. I offer two compelling reasons. First, the founders of WGBH envisioned a place where producers could emphasize excellence over mere acceptability and we have worked hard to nurture this climate.

The second reason is the strong partnership we have forged with you and other New Englanders who believe that outstanding television and radio improve the quality of community life. As a Sustaining Member you are a very special friend because you understand the value of reliable support in securing the future of public broadcasting.

In the coming months I will be sending along to you items that may cross my desk that I think will give you an inside look at the many exciting activities that are underway here. Thank you again for your steadfast support. If you have any questions or concerns about WGBH or the Sustaining Member program please call us at 617-492-2777, x5719.

Sincerely,

Steven M. Bass
Vice President and Manager for Television Stations

The WGBH Sustaining Member Program • Box 200 • Boston, MA 02134-9939 • 617 492 3505

Thank-you letter to a new
monthly donor
Illustration 5.1

thank-you note to a donor who's given to you both, it's easy for that person to recognize shabby treatment for what it is.

In today's fundraising environment, when most organizations must invest in acquiring first-time donors, loyal long-term donors have become increasingly valuable. But to foster loyalty among its donors, a nonprofit must treat them well—valuing them, respecting them, attending to their needs and interests, listening to them, and adopting policies and practices that keep them connected to its work. This is especially true of those donors you hope to recruit into a monthly giving program!

Assuming, then, that you and your colleagues share this donor-friendly attitude, you've got a shot at building a successful monthly giving program. But there are five other essential ingredients you'll need to bring to bear.

2. **Your organization must have an appealing mission.** An organization must provide a potential donor with a compelling reason to give away her hard-earned money. This is always the case for charities needing repeated individual gifts, and even more so in monthly giving programs.

Research has shown that many people make one-time gifts because they're testing to see how an organization responds to them. Others give small amounts just because you happen to hit them at the right time (and might get nothing at any other time). But to attract genuine commitment—to persuade a donor to pledge monthly gifts to you on a continuing basis—your organization must have a vision, a practical plan for realizing it, and either the track record or the inherent credibility to prove its practicality.

As in any fundraising program, the most important factor in an individual's decision to give on a monthly basis is the simple fact that he was *asked* to do so. But the second most important factor is the appeal of your mission. Your challenge is to convince the donor he is giving to a dynamic cause for which his donation will make a difference. You communicate this message in a simple, direct manner, appealing both to the heart and to the mind. You must inspire a prospect with an action-oriented case, making him believe that money invested in your cause is money well spent. And be sure you write your case for giving from the *donor's* perspective, not obscured by jargon or institutional considerations.

An eight-page, full-color monthly newsletter
published for monthly donors
(this page and next)
Illustration 5.2

THE 700 CLUB FEBRUARY HIGHLIGHTS

4 Cross of Redemption — Be sure to see this inspiring interview with former gang member, and subject of the famed book and film *The Cross and the Switchblade*, **Nicky Cruz**. Now a noted evangelist and author, he'll share why Jesus is the answer for youth survival in today's violent society.

6 Holy Boldness — Stop, look, listen! Tune in to hear and meet the two youngest siblings of the renowned Winans singing family dynasty. **Angie and Debbie Winans** tackle moral issues facing today's youth with their latest album, *Bold*; a musical statement with holy fierceness.

12 There Is Hope! — Discover new hope, as thought-provoking international speaker and author, **Myles Munroe**, shares dynamic insights on how to find hope in a world filled with hopelessness.

20 Wrestling With Faith — Hear how Worldwide Wrestling Federation's "Million Dollar Man," **Ted Dibiase**, started winning the wrestling match of his life, when he stopped wrestling with doubt and completely surrendered to Christ.

23 You Can't Take It With You — Don't miss this enlightening interview with radical financial consultant and author, **Stephen Pollan**. He'll discuss his latest book, *Die Broke*, and explain why he recommends people to, "Exit life as you came into it — penniless!"

Guest schedules are subject to change without notice.

Nicky Cruz

Angie & Debbie Winans

Stephen Pollan

PARTNERS & FRIENDS PLEASE PRAY
For CBN's Worldwide Ministry

Training Chinese Pastors
Partner support is being used in China to train pastors and leaders with a goal of starting 60,000 cell churches. Please pray that God will raise up men and women of courage and integrity to take part in this dramatic evangelistic endeavor.

Evangelists Target Indian Cities
Pray for the 52-week TV series, *Life of Christ*, that partner gifts are helping to air in 12 target cities in India. Ask the Lord to grant good health and safety to the follow-up evangelistic teams, and for a harvest of souls in this unreached part of the world.

ACLJ Centers
Please intercede for the leadership at the American Center for Law and Justice — part of the CBN family of ministries — as they open new centers across the country. Pray that the Lord would guide them as they protect our religious freedoms.

Latino Gospel Blitz
Thanks to CBN partner support, the Latino *700 Club* recently conducted a series of Gospel blitzes throughout Latin America. Ask God to raise up partnering ministries and volunteers to follow up on those who received salvation or requested Christian literature.

Our Internet Address Is:
http://www.cbn.org

3. **You must communicate your message effectively.**

    A few years ago I was hired by a nonprofit organization whose "case statement" was 32 pages long! It took a lot of work with this academic-led organization to convince them that no one would take the time to read or understand their case—even staff and board members!

    Not surprisingly, the organization was having a tough time raising money. The case statement was symptomatic of the leadership's fuzzy thinking and demonstrated their inability to communicate a clear, strong reason for giving.

    After a lot of hard work, rethinking their goals and setting realistic priorities, they created a succinct case statement, which they've made the basis of all their promotional materials. Today, the organization's donor base is growing rapidly and its monthly giving program is highly profitable.

    Brevity and clarity are essential in donor communications. But your writing must also be simple, powerful, and emotionally engaging. This boils down to telling a story, or creating a letter that reads like one individual's letter to a close friend—and it means writing all your materials at the level of Grades 7 to 9. This doesn't mean that your letter, brochure, or annual report will lack substance—but it does mean you must use short, simple words, short sentences, and short paragraphs. Even if you're a university professor, it is still easier for you to read a letter written at a Grade 8 level, if only because the brain (even a big brain) can process short words and short sentences quickly. (The *Wall Street Journal* is written at a high school level.) As a fundraiser, your goal is to make everything as easy as possible for your donors and prospects. Remember, if they're not reading and absorbing what you write, you'll generate far fewer gifts!

    Effective written communication requires more than words. Typeface, layout, and photos or drawings play a major role too, sometimes dramatically increasing—or depressing—response rates. The most useful book you'll find on the subject of communication and design—the two are intertwined—is *Type and Layout* by Colin Wheildon, published by Strathmoor Press. (See the recommended reading section at the back of this book for details.)

4. **You must have an efficient and responsive "back-end" system.**

    Processing monthly pledges—what I call the "back end"—is often the most difficult challenge for both very small and very large charities.

If creating a monthly billing system seems to be more than you can handle, don't be discouraged. Perhaps you can find a dedicated volunteer who will manage the program. If not, you might consider accepting monthly gifts exclusively via electronic channels—and let someone else do the processing.

Jim Fleckenstein at the Navy Memorial Foundation made a wise decision to enroll monthly donors through EFT only. He knew he could effectively handle the back-end work for an EFT program, but not for a more labor-intensive program.

If you decide to mail monthly statements, you'll have to work harder for your money, contacting your donors each month and motivating them to give . . . again and again. This means sending more than a bill. Maintaining the strong, emotional connection that's necessary to keep people giving monthly also requires some sort of personal message and a reply envelope along with the invoice. You may also include a separate insert that dramatizes some recent event or some special benefit just for monthly givers.

5. **You must be able to thank donors promptly and answer their individual concerns.**

Maximizing income from a monthly giving program means enrolling as many individuals as possible . . . keeping them active for as long as you possibly can . . . upgrading them on a regular basis . . . and (as you'll soon see) converting donors who give by check to forms of electronic giving. Thanking your donors in regular and meaningful ways is essential at every stage in this process because:

- Your donors will like you more and therefore be more likely to join a monthly giving program.

- Thank-yous help donors become multi-givers, enhancing their tendency to join monthly giving programs. When appropriate, thank-you packages may even invite donors to join a monthly giving club.

- A timely thank-you conveys an impression of efficiency. A donor assumes that if you're efficient in processing his gift, then you're also spending it effectively.

- A quick response also demonstrates that you're focused on serving donors' needs.

**ACFS Community
Nutritional Education
and Feeding Scheme**

P O Box 96075, Brixton 2019.

Fundraising No: 01 100291 000 8

Fundraising Committee
CHAIRMAN MR M SHAW
HON TREASURER MR W A M CLEWLOW

WOMEN'S FUNDRAISING COMMITTEE
HON LIFE PRESIDENT MRS H OPPENHEIMER
CHAIRMAN MRS R FARRANT

29 August 1994

Dear Friend

Some people have written or phoned to say ... 'With all that's been promised by our new Government, surely you don't need our help any more'.

But we do!

Simply because <u>there's a huge gap between a promise and the reality</u>.

Our economy has been battered over many years. To build it up again to provide the dignity of a job and food on the table for all our people, will take a long time.

So yes, we still need your help, in the most positive way - to help destitute families get on the road to independence again.

If you've already made your R59 monthly commitment to feeding a poor family, then thank you for your foresight and continued generosity. But if not - may I use this little note to remind you how your R59 can feed a poor family for <u>a whole month</u>; and how it's only friends like you who make it possible.

Yours sincerely

MARTIN SHAW - Chairman

P.S. One little 'thank you' desk calendar has been set aside <u>especially for you</u>. I'd love to send it to you really soon.

From South Africa, a reminder to monthly donors
who missed a payment *(this page and next)*
Illustration 5.3

YES, I want to invest in the future of a family!

| I enclose the completed form authorising a monthly gift of: | **OR** | I enclose my one time gift of: |

I enclose the completed form authorising a monthly gift of:

☐ **R59** to provide 1 food parcel

☐ **R118** to provide 2 food parcels

☐ **R177** to provide 3 food parcels

☐ **R**_____ (Any other amount)

Please make cheques payable to ACFS

FROM:

Mr. John Q. Demanet

X1 Blyndon Ct

Jabuwood

5432 UMTATA

OR

I enclose my one time gift of:

☐ **R59** to provide a parcel of essential foodstuffs for a family who doesn't have enough to eat

☐ **R118** to provide 2 food parcels

☐ **R177** to provide 3 food parcels

☐ **R**_____ (Any other amount)

ACFS Community Nutritional Education and Feeding Scheme

PO Box 96075
BRIXTON 2019
Fundraising No. 01 100291 000 8

COMMUNITY NUTRITIONAL EDUCATION — ACFS

1016

Please correct your address details if necessary.

AD94 BAA N373249

If you are sponsoring by Credit Card or Debit Order, please return both <u>this</u> Sponsorship form <u>and</u> the completed Authority Form.

| **Authority for donation by CREDIT CARD OR DEBIT ORDER to ACFS** PO Box 96075, Brixton 2019 | FROM: (ACCOUNT HOLDER'S NAME AND ADDRESS) |

MR/MRS MISS/OTHER	INITIALS	SURNAME

SPONSORSHIP NUMBER
AD94 BAA N373249

ADDRESS:

POSTAL CODE:

TELEPHONE: HOME   WORK

I wish to sponsor the amount of R.......................... on the 5th of .... 1994 and each month thereafter.

EITHER: by Visa/Master Card No:

☐☐☐☐ ☐☐☐☐ ☐☐☐☐ ☐☐☐☐

OR: by Debit Order on my Bank/ Building Society

Expiry Date
☐☐☐☐

*Account No.: ....

Bank/Building Society ....

Branch Name & Address ....

....

City/Town ....

Branch Code ....

I/We authorise ACFS to debit the amount of the donation specified against my/our bank current account or building society transmission account or Visa/Master Card account as indicated.
Receipt of this authorisation by you shall be regarded as receipt thereof by my/our Bank/Building Society.
I/We understand that the monthly withdrawal(s) hereby authorised will be processed by the computer ACB Magnetic Tape Service or card administration which will provide me/us with details of each withdrawal on my/our bank statement or on an accompanying voucher and agree to pay any bank charges relating to this Debit Order or card donation.
ACFS is entitled to the donated amounts legally withdrawn in terms of this authority from my/our account while this authority is in force until I/we notify you at your address in writing of the cancellation of this authority.

Card/Account holder's signature

_____

DATE: ....

* Note: A cancelled cheque should be attached for bank identification purposes

Thanking donors is one of the best ways to reward them. Thanking a donor on the anniversary of her first monthly gift—or for her five or ten years of continuous giving—are great ways to strengthen a donor's bond with your organization.

6. **You need an integrated approach to building a donor program.** There are many ways to recruit members to a monthly giving program:

- direct mail
- person-to-person
- telemarketing
- special events
- space ads
- television
- annual reports

You need to determine which of these channels you'll use—and look for ways they can reinforce one another. Ideally, you'll make use of several recruitment channels (for example, direct mail and space ads supplemented by telemarketing)—and integrate the whole effort into your organization's overall fundraising program.

A client of mine once wanted to develop a monthly giving program but wouldn't allow me to soft-sell the program with an option box on the response devices in their mailings to the house file. I was refused permission even to add a statement along the lines of "For more information on our monthly giving program, please check here." The client would only run a monthly donor promotional ad in its newsletter once a year and send special recruitment appeals. Clearly, this was not the best strategy to build a large monthly giving program!

CHAPTER 6
How to set up a compelling monthly giving program

I have to make a confession. (Even lapsed Catholics in therapy still feel the impulse!) In 1987 I developed Oxfam-Canada's first special monthly donor recruitment package. Despite "knowing better," I mailed the costly package to the entire file of 38,000 donors—without testing it!

I was sure the package would be effective, because I'd designed it to reflect the interests and goals of Oxfam donors—and the package went only to donors, not prospects. I knew our donors wanted their money directed to long-term projects that "help people help themselves," not short-term "band-aid" solutions. So, to capture donors' attention, I designed a package with a Band-Aid(™), still in its wrapper, visible through a TV-shaped window on the envelope front. Our mailing house staff glued each Band-Aid inside, by hand. We identified Oxfam in the upper left-hand corner, and we put two live stamps on the reply envelope (a rarity in Canada or the U.S. in 1987).

My Band-Aid(™) letter from 1987 that
pulled hundreds of new monthly donors
Illustration 6.1

I'm proud to become a SHAREPLAN Donor!

On the first day of each month, I authorize Oxfam-Canada to receive the following donation from my account:

☐ $15   ☐ $20   ☐ $30 ($1 a day)   ☐ $ ▢_____ other

Please enclose a blank cheque marked "VOID". (see reverse side for explanation)

Signature _____

Mr. John Q. Doe
1234 West Elm Street
Major City, USA 00000

Sorry, I can't become a **SHAREPLAN** donor at this time, but I'm enclosing a gift of $ _____

Oxfam National Office,
251 Laurier Ave. W., Ottawa, Ont. K1P 5J6

Through SHAREPLAN you can:

- help put contributions to work faster
- reduce Oxfam's mail costs to increase overseas help
- forget about stamps and cheque writing
- provide regular predictable overseas aid

It's convenient for you! All it takes is one signed form to make sure your generosity has the maximum impact.

Helping Oxfam:

Oxfam-Canada is helped in two ways.

1. Overhead is reduced because processing costs are lower. It may not be much per gift but it adds up. And the savings go to development projects where they are most needed.

2. A regular flow of funds is assured, unaffected by any interruptions, helping our project partners to plan their work.

How you can participate in Shareplan:

1. Complete the authorization form on the other side.

2. Enclose a blank cheque to be used by the bank for verification. Be sure to write "VOID" across the cheque.

3. Mail the form and voided cheque to Oxfam in the enclosed envelope.

The Oxfam Canada guarantee to every Shareplan donor:

You maintain complete control of your donation. If you ever wish to cancel or alter your gift simply call (416-961-3935) and ask for the Shareplan co-ordinator or write or call any Oxfam office.

You will receive an annual report, your tax-deductible receipt for each year's donation and a special newsletter.

Thankyou for joining SHAREPLAN!

Band-Aid(TM) package reply form
Illustration 6.2

The outcome?

The Band-Aid package yielded a higher profit than any other in the history of the organization. One-time gifts alone gave it the highest percentage response in years! As is often the case with a highly successful package, we also received many complaints, ranging from "send the Band-Aid overseas" to "you're wasting good stamps." (Jerry Huntsinger once wrote that there is often a direct correlation between the number of gifts and the number of complaints. I've noticed this as well. I assume it's because people are moved emotionally and feel the need to respond one way or another.)

Oxfam CANADA

National Office • 251 Laurier Avenue West, Suite 301, Ottawa, Canada K1P 5J6 · Tel: (613) 237-5236

April 15, 1987

Dear Oxfam Donor,

You may wonder why there's a band-aid on your reply form... well, it's there for two reasons. One, to get your attention; and two, to point out that your gifts to Oxfam have more than a "band aid" effect -- they're _more_ than temporary solutions.

Many Oxfam donors have found a superb way to make their donations have an even greater effect.

I'm referring to our SharePlan donors.

They've decided if they can donate $10 or $20 or more in one month, it's not beyond their resources to give a similar gift every month.

Coming on a monthly basis, the regularity of such gifts helps Oxfam make long-term plans for long-term development projects.

I'm writing in the hope that you, who already do so much to help others through your donations, will accept this invitation to become a SharePlan donor.

People who have chosen to become SharePlan donors are sending a steady, predictable stream of help to people around the world -- people struggling to make better lives for themselves and their children.

In plain words, if we know your gift is coming each month, and how much you'll send, we can plan better. And make commitments to our project partners. In this way _your help is worth even more!_

Contributing $20 a month comes to about 66 cents a day. Here are a few examples of what Oxfam can do with your help as a SharePlan donor at that level:

1) You can provide all the hoes, picks and other implements for a vegetable garden in Nicaragua big enough to feed dozens of war-displaced refugees.

2) You can fund a year's supply of life-saving

(over, please)

...tive medical care for an ...Salvador.

...enough seeds for people in an African village to harvest over 30 acres of corn. That's enough corn to feed a typical community for more than one year!

You can do these things for 66 cents a day provided regularly through SharePlan. Each month your bank automatically sends your gift to Oxfam. It's simple for you. And your gift gets to work faster!

Our SharePlan donors tell me they feel good knowing they've made a regular commitment to the long-term task of helping people around the world.

Please let me know soon as possible if you can become a SharePlan donor of $20 a month. Or at any amount you choose.

If you like the idea of SharePlan but can't make such a commitment now, I sincerely hope you'll contribute with your usual generosity in any case.

A gift like your last one will be most welcome! Every time you help, the dollars you send are used to help poor people change their lives. It's part of our pledge to you, the one who makes our work possible, that no gift will be a "band-aid" gift.

Thanks to you, we work for long-term solutions.

I hope you'll accept this invitation to become more deeply involved in Oxfam's work. I look forward to hearing from you as soon as possible. Thank you very much for reading this letter, and thank you for all your help.

Sincerely yours,

Meyer Brownstone
Chairperson
Oxfam-Canada

P.S. When you join SharePlan you'll get an annual tax-receipt and special newsletter. Most importantly, you'll know every day of the year you're helping people. Please use the enclosed reply form and envelope and let me hear from you today. Thank you.

This Band-Aid (TM) package helped the client "brand" their "long-term development" program
Illustration 6.3

I know now that I made two mistakes in making that package, despite its success. I probably had some donors downgrade their annual giving because we didn't segment the file according to the last gift or cumulative annual giving. And I should have tested it, especially because it was so expensive to produce—double our normal package cost at that time. As a result, I probably didn't maximize the return from that package.

Fortunately, I had two things going for me:

- My gut instincts (backed by—at the time—ten years of fundraising experience); and

- Solid research that revealed our donors' concern about long-term development.

Now, I don't want to suggest I don't trust my instincts. But I believe it was the research on our donor's interests that made this a success.

The starting-point: research

Raising money—or creating a monthly donor program—without conducting research is like trying to build a house without blueprints.

It is sometimes said that research is what you do before you spend a lot of money, and testing is what you do afterwards. Good research will help you develop your most viable offer. To a fundraiser, research means:

- *Understanding who your donors are.* When you know who they are, you'll know how to effectively communicate with them. You'll discover where they live (more than just an address), what they read, their religious affiliation, etc. You'll be able to compile demographic, psycho-graphic, and behavioral pictures of your donors.

- *Understanding their giving patterns.* When you analyze how they give—dollar amount, recency, and frequency—you'll be able to select the best prospects for a monthly giving club. You can also look to the types of appeal they respond to and tailor your monthly invitations accordingly.

- *Understanding why they give to your organization.* You can discover what motivates a single-gift donor versus a monthly donor, and you can shape future offers around this valuable information to convert more single-gift donors to monthly pledgers.

- *Finding which outside lists produce a higher proportion of monthly donors than others.* For instance, you may find that your local environmental activist organization is a marginal prospect list, but it supplied a disproportionate number of individuals who later became monthly donors to your cause. Since these individuals have such a great Long-Term Value, you may decide to test other environmental lists, and continue using what originally seemed to be a marginal list.

Research comes in two flavors: primary and secondary. Primary research may be either *qualitative* or *quantitative*. Qualitative research (including onc-on-one interviews and focus groups) always involves smaller numbers and more in-depth information gathering. Quantitative research (larger numbers) may be done by mail or phone.

Secondary research involves sifting through other information that has been compiled, analyzed, or published elsewhere. It may be found in publications such as academic journals or in published government research and statistics. Some direct marketing and fundraising periodicals provide valuable second-hand research. (The newsletter *Inside Direct Mail*, formerly *Who's Mailing What!*, is particularly helpful. See the Reading List for more information.) Another form of secondary research, collecting direct mail samples, can be invaluable, because packages that work are mailed again and again.

Both primary and secondary research are indispensable when launching a monthly giving program. You must "know" your audience before you invite them to make such a big commitment: their gender, age, income, giving history, and any other relevant information you can obtain about them. The more you know about the demographics and psycho-graphics of your target audience, the higher your response rate is likely to be.

In designing a monthly giving program, you'll probably find that it's useful to gather the following information and analyze it closely:

- samples of all of the organization's mailings from the previous three years
- information on the segments mailed
- what kind of statistical results they yielded

This way, you can determine which themes or projects did well and which did poorly. You can recognize patterns and identify the elements that seemed to have the most powerful impact on your donors.

On the basis of these observations—and of other, solid research findings—you can design a monthly giving program calculated to be compelling to your prospects.

TEMPORARY MEMBERSHIP CERTIFICATE

THE TIYOSPAYE CLUB

MR. PAUL KARPS

is a member of
THE TIYOSPAYE CLUB

A caring and sharing fellowship of those who belong to
the Extended Family of the Indian children at St. Joseph's
Indian School.

Bro. David Nagel

St. Joseph's Indian School, Chamberlain, SD 57326

Mr. John Q. Doe
1234 West Elm Street
Major City, USA 00000

2150050.-037

Please Return Lower Section

Start a New Tradition of Hope and Prosperity
for Needy Sioux Children: 2150050.-037
Become A Tiyospaye Club Member

☐ Yes, I want to improve — and even save — the lives of poor and abused
children by activating my St. Joseph's Tiyospaye Club Membership.

☐ Enclosed is the first of my monthly gifts of:
     ☐ $15   ☐ $20   ☐ Other $ _____

☐ Please send my enamel Tipi pin, monthly newsletters, biographical
information, and correspondence from the children.

☐ Sorry, I am unable to join at this time.

Enclosed Is my Gift of $ _____

Mr. John Q. Doe
1234 West Elm Street
Major City, USA 00000

Response device from a monthly giving
invitation package *(this page and next)*
Illustration 6.4

Chances are, you'll have the greatest success with a specially named monthly giving club.

Creating a giving club: the watchword is exclusivity

A gift club's name is important to set the proper tone. Names my clients have used successfully include Circle of Friends, Friends for Life, Pledge Partners, SharePlan, and Leadership Circle. But don't just go public with the first clever name that comes to mind. Test the club name. Call 100

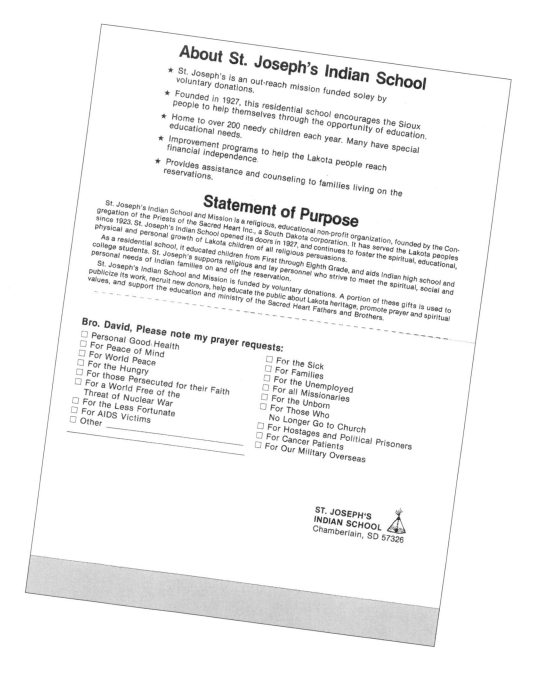

About St. Joseph's Indian School
★ St. Joseph's is an out-reach mission funded soley by voluntary donations.
★ Founded in 1927, this residential school encourages the Sioux people to help themselves through the opportunity of education.
★ Home to over 200 needy children each year. Many have special educational needs.
★ Improvement programs to help the Lakota people reach financial independence.
★ Provides assistance and counseling to families living on the reservations.

Statement of Purpose
St. Joseph's Indian School and Mission is a religious, educational non-profit organization, founded by the Congregation of the Priests of the Sacred Heart Inc., a South Dakota corporation. It has served the Lakota peoples since 1923. St. Joseph's Indian School opened its doors in 1927, and continues to foster the spiritual, educational, physical and personal growth of Lakota children of all religious persuasions.
As a residential school, it educated children from First through Eighth Grade, and aids Indian high school and college students. St. Joseph's supports religious and lay personnel who strive to meet the spiritual, social and personal needs of Indian families on and off the reservation.
St. Joseph's Indian School and Mission is funded by voluntary donations. A portion of these gifts is used to publicize its work, recruit new donors, help educate the public about Lakota heritage, promote prayer and spiritual values, and support the education and ministry of the Sacred Heart Fathers and Brothers.

Bro. David, Please note my prayer requests:
☐ Personal Good Health
☐ For Peace of Mind
☐ For World Peace
☐ For the Hungry
☐ For those Persecuted for their Faith
☐ For a World Free of the Threat of Nuclear War
☐ For the Less Fortunate
☐ For AIDS Victims
☐ Other _____

☐ For the Sick
☐ For Families
☐ For the Unemployed
☐ For all Missionaries
☐ For the Unborn
☐ For Those Who No Longer Go to Church
☐ For Hostages and Political Prisoners
☐ For Cancer Patients
☐ For Our Military Overseas

ST. JOSEPH'S INDIAN SCHOOL
Chamberlain, SD 57326

Tens of thousands of families and individuals faithfully support Bread for the World with membership contributions and special gifts. By writing and calling their Senators and Representatives, members of Bread for the World *are* a powerful citizens' movement on behalf of poor and hungry people.

In the last year, there has been a dramatic shift of power in Congress — exactly at a time when the number of poor people in the United States has grown to a record 38 million Americans *and* starvation threatens the lives of 20 million people in Africa.

Bread for the World and Bread for World Institute together stand as one of the few voices for justice and compassion in this troubling period. More than ever before, this Christian citizens' movement is counting on its members to provide significant financial support — through their participation in one of the following leadership societies.

In addition to their special gifts, members of these societies are asked to:

- Affirm that ending hunger must become a priority for our nation's domestic and foreign policies
- Encourage friends, relatives, colleagues and others to commit themselves to help make hunger a thing of the past
- Remember the needs of poor and hungry people in your prayers

In appreciation for your leadership support, you will receive:

- Special briefing reports about Bread for the World's work on Capitol Hill and around the country
- Free copies of new publications and resource materials

- Your Bread for the World newsletter via first class mail
- Invitations to Bread for the World events in the capital and around the country

President's Circle

The President's Circle enables Bread for the World's president to recognize those individuals who provide exceptional financial support for the organization's activities and programs. Through financial support and leadership involvement, members of the President's Circle encourage renewed commitment to our mission on behalf of poor and hungry people.

When you contribute $10,000 or more annually to Bread for the World or Bread for the World Institute, you'll receive recognition in our annual report as a member of the President's Circle. If you wish, you may attend meetings of the board of directors and participate in special briefings with Bread for the World's senior staff here in Washington, D.C.

**David Beckmann
President
Bread for the World**

David Beckmann consults regularly with each member of the President's Circle through letters, phone calls, and visits throughout the year. The President's Circle is also invited to join the Founder's Society for an annual gathering in the nation's capital. In past years, Members of Congress have participated

Founder's Society

The Founder's Society of Bread for the World was established to express appreciation for the early leadership of Arthur Simon, founder and president from 1975 to 1991. The Founder's Society plays a central role in sustaining Bread for the World's vision of a world where all people have a right to food.

As a member of the Founder's Society, you will be recognized in our annual report. Each year, the Founder's Society gathering in Washington, D.C., will give you an opportunity to meet with Bread for the World's president and senior staff. Other leaders in the hunger movement — from Congress, the Administration and the church — will participate in these special gatherings.

In 1974, Arthur Simon founded Bread for the World while serving as a Lutheran pastor on Manhattan's Lower East Side. He served as the organization's first executive director and later, until 1991, as its president. Simon has been the recipient of many awards, including, in 1990, the Presidential End Hunger Award for Lifetime Achievement. In 1989, on behalf of Bread for the World, he received the Alan Shawn Feinstein Award for the Prevention and [ ] of World Hunger.

Optional payment plans
offer donors convenience
(this page and next)
Illustration 6.5

Bread for the World

President's Circle
Founder's Society
National Associates
Full Harvest Members

For more than two decades, individuals and families have generously supported the work of Bread for the World and Bread for the World Institute. Now there are additional opportunities for you to receive recognition and become more involved in the leadership of this citizens' movement.

PHOTO © BOB CANNON / BREAD FOR THE WORLD

How you can fulfill your Founder's Society commitment

- An annual single gift of $2,500 or more
- A monthly pledge of $200 or more (using either our Autogive program or our monthly reminder system)
- A pledge of $625 each quarter or two gifts of $1,250 each year
- An annual gift to Bread for the World Institute of securities or other appreciated property valued at $2,500 or more

National Associates

National Associates provide annual support of $1,000 or more. Their generous financial support complements the work of thousands of Bread for the World members who provide broad political clout and lobbying influence.

Your leadership support will be recognized in our annual report, which is distributed to political and business leaders, as well as to church agencies and foundations that join you in underwriting our efforts.

How you can make your National Associate's gift

- An annual single gift of $1,000 or more to either Bread for the World or Bread for the World Institute
- A monthly pledge of $85 or more (using either our Autogive program or our monthly reminder system)
- A pledge of $250 each quarter or two gifts of $500
- An annual gift to Bread for the World Institute of securities or other appreciated property valued at $1,000 or more

Bread for the World lobbies Congress on behalf of poor and hungry people, so contributions are not tax-deductible. You may make tax-deductible gifts to support the research and education work of Bread for the World Institute. Please make out your check accordingly.

Individuals and families may also realize significant tax savings by contributing appreciated stock and securities to Bread for the World Institute, or by establishing charitable gift annuities.

Full Harvest Members

The annual contributions of Full Harvest Members total $500 or more. This special level of support helps provide a financial cornerstone for Bread for the World's long-term efforts to change our nation's policies to help end hunger and poverty in the U.S. and around the world.

When you become a Full Harvest member you will receive a copy of Hunger 1996, *Countries in Crisis.*

How you can become a Full Harvest Member

- A single gift of $500 or more — either to renew your membership or as a special contribution
- Join our Autogive program with a pledge of $40 or more per month
- Membership and special gifts that total $500 over the course of the year

PHOTO © RICK REINHARD

In October 1972, a group of Protestants and Catholics met in New York City to explore how persons of faith could be advocates for hungry people. This small group has grown to a national movement of over 44,000 people — with 2,500 volunteer leaders across the country.

Reflecting a variety of religious traditions, Bread for the World members are sustained by the biblical message of hope and justice for all people. Bread for the World does *not* provide direct relief or development assistance. Rather, its members lobby Congress and the Administration to bring about changes in our nation's policies — changes that address the *root causes of hunger and poverty* in the United States and overseas.

In 1992 and 1993 Bread for the World conducted legislative campaigns for the reform of foreign aid generally and the increase of assistance to Africa specifically. In recent years, Bread for the World has sought to protect crucial aid to Africa.

Because of the dramatic change in Congress, Bread for the World has now redoubled its efforts to persuade the Administration and Congress to maintain cost-effective, time-tested domestic nutrition programs. These time-tested programs, like Women, Infants, and Children (WIC), are an essential safety net for the one out of four U.S. children who now live in poverty and face the threat of hunger.

Bread for the World
National Capital Office
1100 Wayne Avenue, Suite 1000
Silver Spring, MD 20910
Phone: (301) 608-2400
Fax: (301) 608-2401

donors or prospects, and ask them which of three choices most appeals to them. A recent phone test pulled in 3 responses for one name, 18 for a second, and 79 for the third—a significant difference. Needless to say, the organization opted for the winner.

I usually design a special logo and letterhead for a monthly giving program, along with special outer envelopes. Typically, I reach for an upscale look, since I want to ensure that donors feel they've been upgraded. In any case, a monthly giving invitation—and other materials from and about the program—should have a distinctive look and feel, different from the normal correspondence with your donors.

The proposition you present to prospective monthly givers—whether in a letter, on the phone, or by any other means—must convey a sense of importance. After all, you're asking for a long-term commitment. You have to get across how the donor's participation in your monthly giving program will be essential to fulfilling your organization's mission. Make your prospects feel very special. Since they will likely be some of your better donors and not just one-time givers, you want to recognize their history of loyal and generous giving and their special commitment to your cause. You want to acknowledge that you've selected them because they care so very much.

The tone of your copy must be personal and warm, yet communicate urgency. Use short words and short sentences. Avoid jargon—or any language—that may slow down or confuse the average reader.

The length of a monthly giving invitation letter can range from one to six pages. Obviously, if you can write a shorter letter and generate an equal response, you'll save money (and be kinder to the environment). I've had great success with two-page letters. However, I believe that, as is usually the case in direct mail, longer copy generally works better. But remember, since you are directing this package to committed donors, you generally need less space to sell your cause: They're already committed.

Concentrate on the strongest selling points:

- Why it's important to join your club right now;
- Why a donor's membership in the club will make an incredible difference to helping your cause further a worthy mission;
- The convenience to the donor;
- Where the donor's money will go—be as specific as possible about this. The more specific you are, the more likely you'll obtain regular gifts. But don't get lost in inconsequential details! Only when you tap into donors' emotions can you recruit them as life-long partners in your monthly giving program!

Clarify your offer

You must be specific and clear about what you're offering. For example:

- Will you accept only monthly donors, or will you give individuals the option of paying on a quarterly basis?

- Will you offer the option of sending a single gift? (My own feeling is that offering the single-gift option significantly reduces the impact of the special invitation. I suggest you do *not* offer this way out—although it might be worth a test.)

All such questions must be methodically considered—and answered—before you invite a single donor to join your monthly giving program.

To think through your plans for monthly giving, use this eight-step process:

STEP 1:

Select the right *"product"* to offer your donors.

Ultimately, your organization's mission is the "product" you're "selling." For example, if yours is an environmental organization with multiple programs, such as protecting endangered rainforests abroad and endangered wildlife in your own country, there are at least two products you could promote: saving an acre of rainforest by giving $25 a month, and supporting a lobbying campaign to protect endangered species, also with a monthly gift of $25.

Finding the best product for your cause is crucial. Through testing, People for the Ethical Treatment of Animals found that a monthly gift for research was the best product option for their donor base.

STEP 2:

Set the *"price."*

More than most other factors, the amount of money you ask for will determine how many people enter your program and how profitable it will be.

You have three pricing options for a monthly giving club:

- A fixed monthly donor level such as $10 or $25

- A list of options such as $10 a month, $20 a month, or $30 a month

- An amount (or amounts) derived from each individual donor's giving history

I prefer the third option. Even if you offer one of the first two options, you should take a donor's giving level and history into account. You should not invite *all* donors into a monthly giving club using a single set of fixed amounts. Instead, I suggest you segment donors into giving categories, say $25 to $99 donors and $100 to $499 donors, with a different Ask for each segment. This will reduce the possibility that a donor will downgrade his annual giving by joining the club.

Most organizations start clubs at $5, $10, or (less often) $20. Ten dollars a month seems to be the most frequent fixed monthly club entry-level. The majority are flexible about the amount donors can give— although they try to discourage monthly gifts below $5.

Some organizations have more than one monthly giving club, with a higher-value offer starting at $50, $100, or even $1,000.

You'll need to decide what's best for your organization. But be sure the amount or range of gifts you request reflects the segment of your donor file you'll be appealing to. For individuals who may have given two or three $10 gifts during a year, you may want to start them at $5 a month but suggest $10 as well. But for someone who has contributed three $50 gifts—an annual giving total of $150—you don't want to give them a $10 entry-level option. I would start with a minimum of $15, offering $20 and $25 as options. This strategy for price-setting would continue all the way up to $1,000 donors, where I advise starting with a $100 minimum suggested monthly gift.

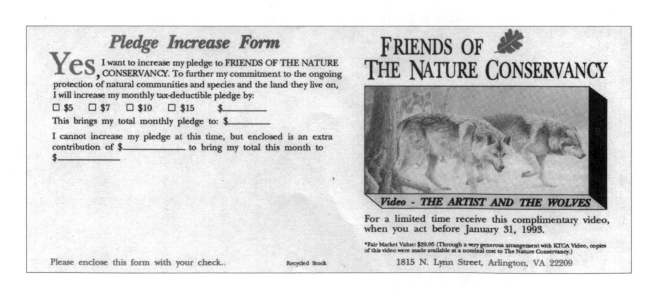

An upgrade offer that includes a video premium
Illustation 6.6

In setting the Ask for prospects, there are two objectives. First, you want to persuade the largest possible number of prospects to join your club. Second, you want to upgrade their annual giving levels (for instance, convincing a habitual $25 donor to send $10 per month). But keep in mind that they're worth far more to you as monthly givers even if they *don't* upgrade: A donor who gives a single gift of $100 each year could give the same amount at $8.33/month.

If all a donor does is spread his typical annual gift evenly over the course of the year, it may appear your organization gains nothing. However, that's certainly *not* true, at least in the case of EFT monthly donors. Such a donor's lifetime of giving is on average two to three times longer than a single-gift donor's, so he's "worth" 200 percent to 300 percent more.

Monthly givers are also easier to upgrade. In asking an $8.33/month donor to upgrade, you might suggest an increase of just 17 cents a day. This sounds reasonable and easily achievable—but over a year it adds up to $60 extra for your organization! That's a 60 percent upgrade—and a commitment to giving that will be sustained much longer.

STEP 3:

Determine the best *offer.*

Your "offer" is the giving option you present to donors to support your "product." In addition to the "price," there are seven other basic considerations when crafting an offer:

1. Do you want earmarked funds, or money for general support? Many donors will give you money without designating where you must spend it. But you may find that your organization can only recruit monthly donors when money is targeted. (You may decide that, even if you could raise 20 percent more money if it's earmarked, you're better off having less money which is unrestricted. Earmarking funds can also cause problems if the campaign that brought donors into the organization's monthly giving club is no longer relevant.)

2. Do you offer a premium to entice a commitment, or to upgrade the average entry-level? Many organizations have found that premium offers are more effective if they are *not* conditional on giving gifts. When donors can accept an offer without feeling compelled to give, then you are building stronger personal relationships with them.

The ideal premium has a high perceived value and a low cost. The premium should offer a benefit or value to the donor or prospect. Ideally, it's linked in an obvious way to the work of your organization, and it has broad enough appeal to increase your response rate. There are endless possibilities. Here are a few:

- a personal family health history booklet from a hospital
- a book that examines issues your organization addresses or solves
- a magazine linked to your cause
- crafts from a self-help project
- a special coffee mug for members
- a booklet of powerful stories telling how your organization helped people
- a video
- engraved plaques, certificates, and membership cards (for donors who actually join your monthly giving club)

You must, however, be cautious. Many donors are sensitive to the possibility that their gifts may be squandered on trifles. This seems to be especially true for environmental causes and other "liberal" causes. In my experience, few donors join a program just to get a premium, then cancel. (But don't offer a free CD player . . . just in case.)

3. Will you offer other, special incentives? For instance, incentives might include free hospital parking, 50 percent off gallery entrance fees, or 25 percent off the price of products in the aquarium's catalog.

4. What payment choices do you offer your donors? Do you only have one option, or two or three choices—EFT, credit card, and monthly statements?

5. Do you provide a guarantee that a donor may change or cancel her commitment at any time? I believe this should *always* be a component of your offer. It will increase the number of people willing to make a commitment. When promoting EFT, it's essential.

6. Do you offer free information on your monthly donor club? This way more people will show an "interest" and provide you with a hot list of prospects with whom you can follow up.

7. Does your offer provide exclusivity, fraternity, or an "insider" feeling? Are you making your club membership attractive to your prospects? Do you emphasize how important their club membership is?

STEP 4:

Select the most cost-effective recruitment *medium.*

If your organization is large and well-heeled, you'll have the luxury of deciding whether to pursue direct mail, telemarketing, television, or other options—or some combination of them. Chances are, however, your choices may be very limited from a practical perspective. (In any case, testing one medium against another can be costly, and it will take a long time to evaluate the results, since the true long-term impact of one versus another may take many years to discern. Only if your program's potential is significant will such testing make sense for you.)

In most cases, I find that monthly giving programs depend largely on direct mail—supplemented, whenever possible, by telemarketing and person-to-person contact. But don't take this for granted: Examine all the options outlined in this book.

STEP 5:

Select the package *format.*

If a direct mail invitation package is at least a central element in your monthly donor recruitment program, what should that package look and feel like?

One packaging approach (design and contents) is likely to be significantly more effective than others in attracting monthly donors to your organization. Yet you have a great many format options. For instance, you might test a small, highly personalized, closed-face package against a 9" x 12" package with an eight-page letter, a color postcard, and a "buckslip" (a small printed insert) that promotes a premium. You face more limitations when you use other media. There may be restrictions that have to do with certain media outlet rules, or technological capabilities. But, in general, your format options are most likely to be restricted by your budget, your imagination, and your boss. In any case, there is always a *best* format for each medium you use.

STEP 6:

Write compelling *copy.*

In a sense, copy and offer are one and the same. However, you may create different copy for each offer. You may also wish to test different *styles* of copy. For instance, you could test a highly emotional appeal versus an offer that's reasoned and elitist. (It's essential that your copy touch people's emotions to spur them on to a response. But there are different emotional triggers. For your cause, being an "insider" may be more important to certain donors than highly charged copy that tells a story of an individual your organization is helping. You'll have to test what's right for your cause.)

When introducing EFT, avoid industry jargon. Even the term "Electronic Funds Transfer" can have negative connotations for some people. You must explain how it works, of course, but de-emphasize the technical aspects.

Some organizations meet the challenge head-on, by giving their programs clear, simple names that convey exactly what the program does. For example, public broadcaster WGBH (Boston) has the "Easy Gift Program." The Gay Men's Health Crisis (New York) has "NOCHEX."

In Canada, "pre-authorized checking"(PAC) is a common term. The highly successful volunteer recruiters for one of my clients refer to themselves as "PAC-rats."

Remember, if you take payment by credit card or check, you'll want a more generic name for the program. EFT then becomes another form of payment, albeit the best.

STEP 7:

Select your best-bet *lists*.

Again, let's assume you'll be using direct mail, at least in part. Fundamentally, there are two lists available to you: The first is your house file, which includes both active and lapsed donors. The second is the large universe of non-donors ("prospect lists"). The distinction between donors and prospects is vital in direct mail and telemarketing. You'll find that donors' individual giving histories will matter, too: Your very best monthly giving prospects are donors who have given frequently and recently. Note that when you use other media, such as television and radio, you end up targeting your recruitment appeal to a broad universe of non-donors—and you have to offer the same message to both donors and prospects.

Monthly Donors

Three year projections for a monthly giving program

Monthly Club	Members	New Members	Average Gift	New Income	TOTAL Income
YEAR ONE					
November	0	0	-	--	
December	15	15	10.00	150.00	150.00
TOTAL	*15*	*15*	*$ 10.00*	*$150.00*	*$150.00*
YEAR TWO					
January	20	5	$10.00	50.00	200.00
February	20	0	$10.00	--	200.00
March	40	20	$10.00	200.00	400.00
April	45	5	$11.00	55.00	495.00
May	50	5	$11.00	55.00	550.00
June	55	5	$11.00	55.00	605.00
July	55	0	$11.00	--	605.00
August	55	0	$11.00	--	605.00
September	55	0	$11.00	--	605.00
October	65	10	$11.50	115.00	748.00
November	85	20	$12.00	240.00	1,020.00
December	105	20	$12.00	240.00	1,260.00
TOTAL	*105*	*90*	*$11.22*	*$1,010.00*	*$7,293.00*
YEAR THREE					
January	115	10	12.00	120.00	1,380.00
February	125	10	12.00	120.00	1,500.00
March	150	25	12.00	300.00	1,800.00
April	165	15	13.00	195.00	2,145.00
May	170	5	13.00	65.00	2,210.00
June	175	5	13.00	65.00	2,275.00
July	185	10	13.00	130.00	2,405.00
August	185	0	13.00	--	2,405.00
September	190	5	13.00	65.00	2,470.00
October	200	10	13.00	130.00	2,600.00
November	220	20	13.00	260.00	2,860.00
December	240	20	13.00	260.00	3,120.00
TOTAL	*240*	*135*	*$12.67*	*$1,710.00*	*$27,170.00*

STEP 8:

Determine the best *times* to mail or phone or air your offer.

You can test a monthly giving invitation:

- by time of year
- at particular points in a renewal cycle
- immediately after a person becomes a new donor
- four to six months after a person becomes a new donor
- on an anniversary of the first gift
- after the second gift
- after the second gift in a year

Each of these times has worked best for at least one of the causes I've worked with. A political party found that the optimum time for its donors to be approached was four months after a first gift. A social service agency had great success inviting people to join a special club immediately after their first gift. And a PBS station found a great time to invite people to join was in the eighth month of their annual membership cycle—just before they started getting renewal notices for the upcoming year. All organizations are different—and many groups of prospects are different from one another. You'll need to test the timing of your invitation.

CHAPTER 7
EFT and credit cards—the keys to loyal monthly giving

Is there life after death? Sometimes, it appears so. In September 1993, a 72-year-old woman in Stockholm was found dead in her apartment when the landlord entered to renovate it. The coroner said the woman had died *three years* earlier.

No one knew she'd died, because her social security pension checks were automatically deposited to her bank account, and her rent, phone bills, and other monthly expenses—including, perhaps, charitable donations—were automatically deducted.

It is, of course, tragic that no one knew this woman had died alone and undiscovered. But her story illustrates a phenomenon familiar to those who work with Electronic Funds Transfer:

Once someone signs on to an EFT program,
she may be making more than a lifetime commitment!

What is EFT?

An Electronic Funds Transfer (EFT) is, simply, a computerized financial transaction. It's one of the few successful examples of the "paperless world" we were once promised.

Donors who make gifts by EFT authorize an amount, a schedule (usually monthly, though sometimes quarterly), and a date on which withdrawals are to be made from their accounts. The withdrawal date is usually the first or fifteenth of the month in Canada. In the U.S., it's often the third, fourth, or fifth, since Social Security checks are deposited on the third. Other programs give donors a choice of a couple of dates.

These transactions occur automatically, without monthly reminders or invoices.

In most of the developed world, EFT is very common:

- More than 80 million electronic transactions take place every day in North America.
- Fifty percent of Canadians use EFT to pay their bills or contribute to charity.
- In Europe, 85 percent of the population uses EFT.
- In Japan, an estimated 95 percent are regular users.

By contrast, only about 5 percent of the U.S. population currently uses EFT. Among the causes: a complicated banking system, and laws that didn't allow EFT until 1979. However, the growth since 1979 has been significant, and it's increasing rapidly. My guess is that by sometime early in the 21st century, at least 30 to 50 percent of Americans will be using EFT. In Britain, direct debit is the common name for EFT donations to charities. Canadian nonprofits and businesses tend to use the terms "pre-authorized payment" (PAP) or "pre-authorized checking" (PAC).

As an alternative, I coined the term "automatic bank transfer" for a U.S. nonprofit that was afraid its elderly donors wouldn't like anything electronic. You're welcome to use it, too!

Most gifts to nonprofits in the U.S. go through the Automated Clearing House (ACH), a private network managed by banks. It was established to allow individuals to make electronic payments to organizations. The ACH system has developed to the point where major organizations, large and small, use it to make payments to individuals.

In many countries, a significant percentage of payroll checks are automatically deposited into employees' accounts through EFT. Governments in many states and countries make social security payments through EFT. As of January 1, 1999, all U.S. Social Security payments became electronic.

Any day now, more than half of North American households will own computers. This will lead to a dramatic increase in the use of online bill-paying. The more this occurs, the more familiar people will be with zipping money in and out of their accounts electronically. And as more people become familiar with automatic debit cards and Internet banking, it becomes easier for them to accept automatic debits going from their accounts to your organization's account.

Donors keep giving with EFT

Electronic Funds Transfer enables organizations to maximize the amount of money they raise, and it provides them with steady, long-term income.

The EFT drop-off rate is so low—usually two to eight percent per year—that many of these donors will go on giving a decade or longer after they first sign up.

Once a donor joins an EFT program, it's much easier to stay on than to drop off. To lapse, you first have to decide to cancel (which is psychologically difficult once you've made a commitment). Then you have to notify the nonprofit, and you may even feel the need to explain your reasons for quitting. In short, people keep giving because of one of the most powerful forces in human history—inertia.

Introducing ...
A new and easy way to help the kids!
(Just for our Monthly Sponsors!)

We thank God every day for Monthly Sponsors like you! Your special commitment means everything to our homeless kids.

Because you mean so much to us, we'd like to do something special for you.

For a long time now, Monthly Sponsors have been asking us for an easier, more convenient way to make their monthly gift. And now ... today ... we've found it. It's our new Automatic Pledge Option.

What is the Automatic Pledge Option?

It's a new pledge service that allows you to pre-authorize your Monthly Sponsor gift to Covenant House. Now you can enjoy the convenience and reliability of having your bank pay your monthly gift. Which means you don't have to write out a check any more ... search for a stamp ... make special trips to the post office.

How does it work?

Actually, your bank does all the work for you. You just let us know how much you want to pledge on a monthly basis, and we'll tell your bank to deduct that amount each month from your checking account. Your donation is reliably sent to Covenant House.

How much should I pledge?

Whatever you feel comfortable pledging. There is no set amount. If you ordinarily like to give $10 a month, just write that amount on your enrollment form. If you can give more, that would be wonderful and would help our kids a lot.

How long does the option last?

The option lasts as long as you want it to. If, at any time, for any reason, you would like to cancel your pledge, all you have to do is notify us. We'll take care of it for you immediately.

How does enrolling in the Automatic Pledge Option help Covenant House?

Of course every time you make a gift, it helps our kids! But this option helps in a special way. It lets us know in advance how much is coming in every month, so that we can prepare early and budget our resources. And, quite honestly, because we don't have to open envelopes and record gifts, it helps to keep our administrative costs low.

When can I enroll?

Right away!

Just check off the box on your enclosed gift slip, sign it, and return it to us. And please include a check for the first month.

The Automatic Pledge Option will begin automatically transferring your donations the second month after you enroll.

More questions?

If there's anything else you'd like to know about how the Automatic Pledge Option works, just call us at

1-800-388-3888

We'll be more than happy to answer any of your questions.

On behalf of our kids, thanks so much for your support.

COVENANT HOUSE
P.O. Box 731, Times Square Station,
New York, NY 10108-0731

Enclosure sent with a statement to monthly check donors promotes EFT
Illustration 7.1

Here's a personal example of inertia:

Two years ago, I authorized a charity to upgrade my monthly gift by $5. A few months later I discovered they had mistakenly upgraded me by $10, and now I'm giving more than I'd authorized. But I've decided it's not worthwhile for me to correct the mistake. I would have to call them—possibly several times, before reaching the right person—and after all, "it's only $5 a month." I figure God intervened and that I really won't miss the extra money each month. The upshot? The charity now withdraws $35 each month from my account, which adds up to an extra $60 per year for them—probably for 40 more years.

However, I do *not* recommend you try double-dipping with your donors! Yes, it's likely that you'd be surprised by the number who would fail to notice, or, even noticing, let you continue taking more money from their accounts. But getting away with something doesn't make it ethical!

Why monthly donors lapse

I've collected letters from people who drop out of monthly giving by EFT. Here are typical reasons they give:

- "Sorry, I have to stop my pledge, but I lost my job six months ago, . . . I'll rejoin when I can."
- "On behalf of Mrs. Smith, I'm writing you to cancel her monthly payment because she has been moved to a nursing home and is no longer capable of managing her affairs."
- "My father passed away, please cancel his pre-authorized payment."
- "I'm moving out of the country (or your geographic area) and therefore wish to cancel."
- "Due to other financial commitments, I'd like to stop my club membership."

As you can see, the reasons people give for cancellation highlight the psychological strength implied by a "pledge," which is, after all, a promise. Unpredictable life transitions are the primary reasons people stop giving:

- losing a job
- returning to school
- reduction in income
- retiring from the workforce
- moving from the service area
- senility or death

People usually cancel their EFT pledges only because of extenuating circumstances. Usually, they still support the nonprofit. In fact, many of these donors will return to the program if their circumstances change—such as finding a job, or recovering from a grave illness.

Most donors will notify you when they cancel, but you may only learn of some decisions when the transactions don't go through. Bob Wesolowski, President of CHI Cash Advance, gave me this breakdown of reasons for non-transfer of gifts to a nonprofit:

- 24%   insufficient funds in account
- 51%   account closed
- 18%   authorization revoked by donor
- 3%   deceased
- 3%   account frozen (legal proceedings, possibly caused by death, divorce, or lawsuit)

Those percentages may be intimidating. Be sure to put them in perspective: Out of tens of thousands of transactions only *three-quarters of one percent* were stopped for the above reasons.

Elderly donors and EFT

An 89-year-old alumnus of a major university was asked by a younger volunteer to join the school's monthly giving program. The volunteer presented the case and then asked for a 12-month pledge. The senior replied, "I'd be happy to make a single gift, my dear, but I can't make a pledge. At my age, I don't even buy green bananas anymore."

The issue of age is important because many of your donors, if not the majority, will be 60 years or older. It's true that some people at a "certain age" refuse to make long-term commitments. Nevertheless, many older donors will become monthly donors, and for that reason it's worthwhile to ask them to pledge. A good tool for seniors is a "Q-&-A" brochure to answer the questions they're most likely to ask.

I'm often told by development directors that EFT sounds like a good idea in theory, but they believe their donor base, primarily older and female, "won't go for it." I've heard this concern from almost every nonprofit I've worked with.

These development directors are partially right, but mainly wrong. Yes, many charities have donor bases that are largely made up of older women. But it's incorrect to assume these women will not make monthly pledges via "modern technology." Donors will join if they believe in your cause.

Remember, many seniors are used to having checks from Social Security and other sources deposited to their accounts by EFT. Some pay bills by EFT. My experience with a wide cross-section of organizations in many countries indicates that many elderly donors are comfortable with EFT and credit card giving to nonprofits.

One of my clients conducted a large survey to discover who was giving to them through EFT. Donors in the 35-44 year age group gave most frequently through EFT. However, donors 65 years and over came a close second! These were also the two top giving segments for all donors to this charity, although in reverse order.

A large religious nonprofit converted 5.5 percent of its elderly donor file to EFT in just over 18 months and 12.5 percent in 30 months. The response of older donors will vary from charity to charity, and there are many other factors that influence their responses—education, for example, and the nature of the cause. My client's survey revealed that people who join these programs tend to be better educated than the average donor and the general population.

Many of your seniors will join an EFT program, and the numbers will grow as EFT is embraced by business. Seniors will have no option but to become more familiar with the concept and the ease of pre-authorized payments.

Finding an EFT vendor

An EFT program is unlikely to burden you or your staff because computers do the heavy lifting. But there's another reason: *Someone else* will probably be doing most of the work.

It's possible for you to manage an EFT system yourself, but there are cost-effective ways to farm out the work, reducing wear and tear on your organization and gaining the full benefit of EFT's built-in efficiencies.

You ultimately have two choices: a bank, or a company dedicated to providing electronic funds services to businesses and nonprofits. In my experience, an EFT supplier is likely to be a much better bet. Companies that specialize in EFT have to be good at it (or at least they should be!), because it's their major business. For banks, EFT tends to be a small profit center and a low priority. Serving your organization's needs may not be at the top of their list.

However, all EFT companies are not created equal. Investigate at least three suppliers of EFT services. (You'll find a list of five following the reading list at the back of this book.) Their competency, range of services, and rates may vary significantly.

For example, here's a sad, cautionary tale . . .

In one recent month, the gifts from a nonprofit's EFT donors were not debited from their bank accounts. Then, in the next month, *two* deductions were made from every donor's account. This slip-up was caused by the vendor . . . so it's worth doing a little work to find the right EFT vendor!

Both the quality and the diversity of services offered will vary significantly, so make sure you conduct a thorough cost/benefit analysis. For example, some EFT services impose a minimum monthly charge, while others do not. Some provide you with detailed analyses of your transactions, others with a minimum of information.

When you check out EFT vendors, keep these tips in mind:

- Talk to their clients and their former clients.

- Ask for "bids" instead of "quotes" (which may save you money).

- Make sure that when you receive a bid, the supplier has specified all costs for transaction fees, uploading names, and all other aspects of the process.

- Make sure you can get free and easy access to your donor data because one day you may want either to change vendors or bring your program in-house. And don't forget to check if there are hidden costs or complications if you decide to switch.

- When one nonprofit compared monthly transaction fees for two EFT service providers, it learned that one of the firms charged 25 percent more. But when all fees and charges were taken into account, that firm's price turned out to be much lower!

When you contact a service provider to solicit a bid, here's what you want to know:

- monthly fees
- set-up fees
- costs for name and address changes and additions
- any other hidden costs
- the turnaround time on your donations (one day, three days, one month?)
- the process by which they enroll donors in the program

- information on how they track donor deposits (ask for samples of tracking sheets)
- what other kinds of reporting and analysis services they provide (ask for samples)
- what makes this vendor's service unique and superior to the competition

You also want to find out what cost differences there are when you start your program. If your first EFT is from only 100 donors, what does that cost?

Tell each supplier that you're comparing its services and fees with other companies. This information will help you obtain more comprehensive information.

One more pointer: Insist on a clause in your vendor or bank contract that ensures that, in the case of any error, the supplier will contact a donor, admit its mistake, and apologize. (Make sure you see—and approve—their apology!) This is important for two reasons: (a) the bank or service bureau will take the blame for something that may irritate the donor, and (b) the service bureau or bank, not you, will pay for the cost of apologizing (although you will probably also want to apologize yourself).

It's Easy to Begin

1. Sign the enclosed Pledge Reminder.

2. Send it in with your check for this month's pledge in the enclosed envelope.

3. We'll do the rest!

Your first **EZ** Pledge gift will be transferred automatically when your next pledge is due.

We sincerely appreciate your Pledge gifts however you choose to support Oxfam America.

Oxfam America

26 West Street, Boston, MA 02111-1206

printed

Help Oxfam America fight hunger and poverty without ever writing another check!

Components of a monthly giving package *(this page and previous)* Illustration 7.2

QU

Please
Pledg

617/728-2

Oxfam A

EZ Pledge

Choose the **EZ** Pledge Option Today!

To make supporting Oxfam America even more convenient, consider the *EZ Pledge* option—available only to Oxfam America's Pledge Partners. When you choose *EZ Pledge* your monthly gifts are transferred automatically by your bank. *EZ Pledge* eliminates check writing and bank check charges.

EZ Pledge *Increases the Value of Your Pledge Gift!*

• Reduces our costs for processing your donations.

• Speeds your gifts without long mail delays.

• Provides Oxfam America with a reliable stream of resources so we can better plan our funding to overseas development projects.

• Saves trees by eliminating monthly reminders.

EZ Pledge

Questions & Answers

Q. Just how does *EZ Pledge* work?
A. You can have a fixed sum transferred from your savings or checking account to Oxfam America's bank account each month. Our system is similar to those used for many fixed payments, such as home mortgages, car loans, and insurance premiums.

Q. How can I increase or decrease my pledge amount or skip a month's pledge using this method?
A. Simply call or write us. Oxfam America will arrange for whatever change you'd like to make.

Q. What record will I have of my month's pledge?
A. Besides your monthly checking account statement showing the date and amount of the transfer to Oxfam America, we will send you a year-end statement listing your contributions for the year.

Q. What if I change my mind?
A. Again, just call or write us if you want to stop the automatic transfers or if you move or change banks.

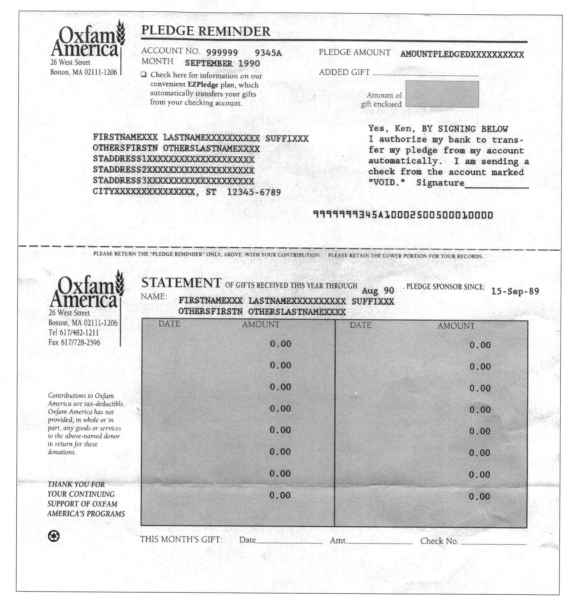

A monthly donor statement, including an effort
to convert a check donor to EFT
Illustration 7.3

What does EFT cost?

EFT costs depend on whether you work with an independent service provider or with a bank. The monthly charge for a transfer is generally between 40 cents and 80 cents per transaction. The cost goes down as the number of transactions goes up.

The set-up fee to establish an account can range from $300 to $1,000, although in some cases no set-up fee is charged. The fee depends on how complicated the program is and whether any additional services are part of the package you're buying.

Bank fees tend to be lower than those charged by independent service providers—often as low as 15 to 20 cents per transaction. However, there are additional, hidden costs involved. For instance, some banks require nonprofits to lease or buy special software or equipment. And a number of charities have found that they simply get better service from independent vendors than from banks.

While a few nonprofits do the banking work themselves, establishing an EFT program is complicated. Many organizations have tried to handle the job themselves, only to give up and hire outside companies to provide the service.

One of the complications: You must match computerized donor records with the system for handling transfers used by each donor's bank. This is better left in the hands of specialists, who are familiar with the terrain and can give you the reports you need at a very low cost.

How much money will you save?

As direct mail and telefundraising costs continue rising through the years, EFT will save you more and more money.

For example, compare the cost of mailing monthly reminders versus EFT. At one major U.S. charity, 3,000 donors received monthly pledge statements. The organization was paying 92 cents to produce and mail each reminder notice to these donors. When all the donors converted to EFT, the organization saved $2,760 a month, or $32,120 a year.

Gay Men's Health Crisis calculated that it was spending 40 cents to handle each gift made electronically, but more than $1 for each check. And this gap will increase as the cost of postage goes up.

You can also save money by sending *less mail* to your monthly donors. Generally, I recommend that you take the monthly EFT and credit card donors out of your normal solicitation stream. (But ask them if they still want to receive all your mailings, anyway. Some will). Let's assume you normally send eight appeals each year to your active donors. You'll save money if you reduce the amount of mail to your monthly donors to three or four pieces a year—perhaps an annual report and a special appeal, plus one or two requests to raise their pledge amounts.

How much will you save? The biggest variable is the number of donors enrolled in your monthly giving program. If you take into consideration the total cost of preparing a direct mail letter, the savings could total $1 per piece. Multiply the number of monthly donors by $4 ($1/piece times four fewer pieces to be mailed). You can see how the savings add up, especially once you recruit thousands of donors to your program!

You might also look at the savings in time and labor. How long does it take one of your staff to process a check? Someone has to open the envelope, check for a signature, match the name and address on the reply form (and perhaps the outside of the envelope as well). That person must verify that the amount written in words matches that written in numbers, then put the pieces together, sort them, and so on. Compare that process to the magic of EFT: Money automatically appears in your bank account!

One of my clients now has a single person managing a monthly giving program supported by more than 6,000 donors. That's 72,000 transactions a year! How many staff members would you need to process 72,000 checks? Equally important, the person managing this sustainer program spends a fair amount of her time building donor loyalty. She has time to attend staff meetings, talk to donors on the phone, and send personal correspondence to donors.

EFT brings you other financial benefits, too

The $32,120 that one U.S. nonprofit saved using EFT works out to $10 per donor per year. Savings were made in processing costs. Deposits and posting costs were virtually eliminated. The possibility of bad checks, and of checks lost in the mail, was significantly reduced.

The group also gets its money *sooner*. If somebody across the country makes an EFT donation to your organization, you should receive it within one to three days. However, you'll wait for weeks as a donor writes and mails a check. Once that check arrives, your staff has to open the envelope, process the donation, and deposit the money. You'll probably lose anywhere from 7 to 21 days' time when that money could be earning interest for your organization.

Why don't all nonprofits have EFT programs?

Too many nonprofits remain wary of EFT because they are stuck in the past. They prefer the things they already know how to deal with. Some feel their donors are too old to learn new tricks, that they'll be suspicious of anyone automatically taking money out of their personal accounts.

In some nonprofits, especially large organizations with a variety of donor programs, the resistance may lie in turf battles. The individuals responsible for these programs often want to protect "their" donors to ensure they meet their financial goals. A successful EFT program will increase your organization's net income overall, but might reduce the income credited to telemarketing or direct mail or to a specific "level of giving." (For instance, a successful monthly giving club is very likely to be attractive to $50 - $125/ year donors.)

Your telemarketing or direct mail consultant may also lay down roadblocks. Many consultants don't recommend monthly giving programs that feature EFT for three reasons:

- The consultant may have no experience with EFT or monthly giving, so she tells the client, "It won't work."

- If you convert a significant number of donors, especially multi-givers into monthly donors, you may well triple their annual giving. But this may reduce the profits from your telemarketing or direct mail programs, and your consultants might not look as good at the end of the year.

- Some consulting firms take a 10-20 percent "commission" from printers or mail houses! This is a questionable practice—and an ethical problem if your organization doesn't know about it. (Ask your consultants where they stand on this question.)

One way to avoid a conflict with your direct response consultant is to establish monthly giving as a component of the direct marketing program. If you and your consultants are focused on the big picture—an overall increase in annual net income (and, of course, enhanced long-term stability)—it shouldn't matter how much comes from which program.

Another way to avoid a conflict is to redefine your approach to direct response fundraising. Think of the process as consisting of *two levels* of prospecting. At ground level, you use direct mail (or telemarketing) to acquire new donors. This costs money. You're willing to pay the cost, because you know the enormous Long-Term Value your organization will realize.

By analogy, you can think about a *second level* of prospecting. At this stage, your goal is to convert single and multi-gift donors to monthly giving. If you look at it from this perspective, launching a monthly giving program may be less likely to cause internal strife.

COVENANT HOUSE
P.O. Box 731, Times Square Station
New York, NY 10108-0731

Gift Slip

"I bound myself by oath, I made a covenant with you ... and you became mine."

Ezekiel 16:8

MONTHLY SPONSOR PROGRAM

❑ **YES, I want to make sure my monthly gift gets to the kids quickly and conveniently.** I have read the terms and conditions and have signed below. I know I can discontinue this service at any time simply by notifying Covenant House.

Pledge Amount: $ _____   Signature: _____   Date: _____

Please fill in the pledge amount, sign your name and date, and return this slip with your check in the enclosed envelope! Please ... make your check payable to Covenant House. Your gift is tax deductible as provided by law. Thank you.

❑ **I *don't* want to try the Automatic Pledge Option** (I like giving the usual way!)
Here's my Monthly Sponsor donation of: $_____.

Terms of Agreement

My authorization to charge my account at my bank shall be the same as if I had personally signed a check to Covenant House.

This authorization shall remain in effect until I notify Covenant House or my bank in writing that I wish to end this agreement, and Covenant House or my bank has a reasonable time to act on it; or until Covenant House has sent me 10 days written notice that they will end this agreement.

A record of my payment will be included in my regular bank statement and will serve as my receipt.

COVENANT HOUSE *Bulletin Board*

You do so much for our kids ... we'd like to do something for you.

To make your monthly giving more convenient, we're starting a new service called the Automatic Pledge Option.

This service lets your own bank make your contribution conveniently every month to Covenant House.

It makes giving easier for Monthly Sponsors like you because you won't have to write out a check every month or look for a stamp. And it helps Covenant House cut down on our administrative costs. All you have to do to enroll in the Automatic Pledge Option is to:

(over, please)

KEEP THIS STUB FOR YOUR RECORDS

I have elected to have my bank pay my monthly pledge to Covenant House. I know I can discontinue this service at any time simply by notifying Covenant House.

My Pledge Amount

$ _____

Date Pledged

_____

COVENANT HOUSE
P.O. Box 731, Times Square Station
New York, NY 10108-0731

A monthly reminder to donors
who send monthly checks
Illustration 7.4

Why do some donors prefer monthly invoices?

Despite the compelling arguments for monthly giving via Electronic Funds Transfer or credit card, some of your donors may prefer you bill them every month. Why?

- They retain a sense of control over their money and their giving.
- They're nervous about anyone having access to their bank accounts.
- They just don't like this 21st century phenomenon of money moving around without their being directly involved—especially when it's *their* money!
- They like the regular communication because they really want to know more about your work, or perhaps they feel lonely.
- They're worried that they may not have enough money in their account and want to control when they send a check.
- They're testing you to see how you treat them.
- They're not as committed as the people who go directly into electronic monthly giving.
- They hate or mistrust banks.
- They know that once you give by EFT, it's harder to stop giving.
- You offer them the option of monthly statements. (If you don't, many may join with EFT or credit card payments despite their misgivings.)

You might also survey the donors who write monthly checks. You may not be able to satisfy all of their concerns—but you *can* confront a number of them successfully. Once you know the reasons, then you can start addressing them in your communications and attempt to convince people to change their mode of giving. We'll explore that topic in Chapter 12.

What your service bureau or bank needs from you

Your service bureau or bank needs six pieces of information for each contribution:

- the customer's name
- the customer's bank's transit routing number
- the customer's account number
- the customer's identification number
- the transaction code
- the amount of the contribution

There are at least three ways to manage the transfer and management of this information:

1. The service provider maintains a file and does all the data entry for you from the manual forms you fill out. This is the best option for most organizations.

2. The service provider holds your file on its computer, but you input all the data online, by modem.

3. You maintain the file, update as necessary, and transmit a copy to the bank or other vendor on the appropriate dates. The choice is yours—but the data-exporting capabilities of some fundraising software are problematic.

Your service provider needs updated information from you at least one or two days before each debit date. (The sooner the better.) To transfer the information, you can send it either by disk, by modem, or by fax. (If you transmit via modem, make sure you have clear instructions.) Sending by modem gives you more time to update donor files, process upgrades, or delete cancellations. If you use disks, you'll lose a day in delivery, and have to pay delivery charges as well.

Once your vendor has updated information in hand, the EFTs can be processed. Here's what happens:

- Each bank deducts gifts from any donor accounts it holds. Then each banksends information about those debits to your organization's bank, so the deductions may be credited to your account.

- Your service provider credits your account on the same date that the deductions are made from the bank accounts. For some service providers, this may take two or three days; in the odd case, longer. If you find that your service provider takes more than one week to provide you with these funds, ask for a quicker transfer. Your money should be transferred almost immediately. Otherwise, the service provider is using your money to earn interest for itself.

- Standard practice: If the organization has an account at the processor's bank, the organization gets next-day money. If they have an account at another bank, the bank is more concerned and delays availability 1-3 days. The bank is concerned that it may get stuck with returns after the organization draws down the donor's funds.

What happens when an EFT bounces?

Every once in a while—about one in 150 transactions—you'll find that a debit fails. This can be due to:

- a stop-payment on the account

- a closed account

- insufficient funds

- a customer has contacted you to revoke his contribution, but too late to catch the actual withdrawal.

Your service provider will charge your bank account when it is notified of a rejected entry. The vendor will then pass the word to your organization by e-mail, paper, fax, or whatever method you've agreed on.

Signing up a donor for Electronic Funds Transfer

Whatever method you use to recruit a donor, you need to get written authorization to debit his or her account. For example, if you've recruited her via television, you must ask her to fill out a form and send it back to you, to make the monthly deposits possible.

There's a big advantage in direct mail and person-to-person recruiting: you can collect a personal check and secure full authorization when the person commits. That way you dramatically reduce the possibility of the donor's reneging on her commitment.

There are five federal requirements for EFT in the U.S.:

- The donor must sign a form that authorizes the transaction.

- The terms must be clear.

- The agreement must specify how much and for how long (or indicate that it will continue until the donor notifies the bank).

- The donor must be free to cancel at any time by contacting the organization.

- The donor must receive a copy or a photocopy of the authorization form. (This is not a requirement in Canada.)

After a donor has committed to your program, you need to look after a few additional details:

1. First, the donor signs a written authorization for your organization to charge his or her account, specifying the amount to be deducted, the date or day of month, and the frequency (monthly, quarterly, or on some other schedule).

2. You send this authorization electronically to the bank or service provider. The bank checks for errors, contacting you to make corrections, if necessary. (This is called a "notification of change," or NOC.) A good service provider can often make corrections without contacting you.

3. After you or the vendor make any necessary corrections on your database, you then send the required information by disk or modem to the bank on the scheduled date.

4. Finally, the bank deducts the agreed amounts on the agreed date or dates.

5. Yes, this may be boring but it's important for you to know: Make sure you give each of your new sustainers a *unique ID number*. This is crucial. Otherwise, you're bound to experience problems finding donors, updating records, and maintaining a smooth relationship with your service provider. But try to keep the ID number short so your donor doesn't feel like a number.

Stopping a payment

Every donor has the power to stop his EFT payment at any time—and you must emphasize this in all your promotional material. Donors won't be willing to give you access to their bank accounts without knowing exactly how they can cancel the arrangement.

Some organizations ask for cancellation in writing, while others accept it over the phone. Legally, the cancellation may have to be in writing. However, if a donor calls you to cancel don't ask him to put his wishes in writing. It's a waste of time for him, and it feels like unfriendly service on your part.

In some cases, you might want to verify a telephone cancellation if you think someone else canceled a donor's monthly payment. Have a senior person in your organization call the donor to verify it, with the thrust of the call being to thank them for all they've done and "sorry, we'll miss you." This call is an opportunity to ask if there was some specific reason for the cancellation. Knowing why a donor canceled his pledge will be very helpful when you try renewing him sometime in the future.

A donor may also challenge an EFT transfer within 60 days by making a written statement to his bank. There are four valid reasons for this:

▪ The donor had not authorized a direct payment.

▪ The authorization was withdrawn.

- The amount was incorrect.
- The amount was debited on the wrong day.

If a donor challenges a deduction, the best policy is to refund his money—immediately. This gives the donor the all-important sense of control over his account and his gifts to you. It also will save you from a potentially time-wasting dispute that might give the donor a bad feeling, and possibly even produce negative media coverage.

If you send the refund yourself, your auditing department will have to mail a check. That may take a while. A good service provider can get the refund out that same day.

How to set up a monthly giving program for your organization

You have two choices: Hire an expert, or do it yourself. A consultant should be able to save you time and money. (I will!) He should also point you in the right direction, based on his experience in developing other programs.

If you decide to set up the program yourself, begin by getting a team of people to research what similar organizations are doing and to evaluate various service providers. Your team might include people responsible for finance and accounting, direct marketing, and customer service. You may want to contact an expert on monthly donor programs to help you figure out how much it will cost to develop the program.

Once you've done the research, get some feedback within your organization. If you have regular full staff meetings, take the opportunity to introduce EFT. Explain its benefits and encourage staff members to use this method to give to your cause.

It's important to get accounting involved. While you look at revenue, they look at costs. They often have the authority to kill a program if they aren't happy or consulted early.

Some individuals may be concerned about losing their jobs if a lot of gift processing is done automatically. Of course, this depends on how large your organization is, but these are issues that must be dealt with. I have one client that receives approximately 140,000 gifts a year, more than half by EFT. In this case, because the overall fundraising program grew along with the EFT program (although not nearly as fast), no jobs were lost.

If your organization is like most nonprofits, there's never a shortage of work to do, just a shortage of funds. And since this kind of program will bring in more money, there won't likely be any job loss.

By this point, you should already be thinking about who will manage the program. If you use a service bureau, then you probably don't need to hire additional staff, just shuffle the responsibilities of existing staff members. If your program is very large, you may decide to hire a new person or promote someone on staff to this very important position. The qualifications required include excellent attention to detail and strong interpersonal skills, because this person will probably communicate with monthly donors by phone and letter.

The next step is to select a service provider or bank. They can help train the appropriate staff members. Training is important, because you may discover that your staff will have to explain EFT to your donors. It's essential that everyone be familiar with the basics, especially the advantages to both the donor and the organization.

While you're busy training and informing your staff, you also have to:

- Investigate what hardware or software you may need to handle the data. Plan how you will process the authorization forms.

- Determine the layout of the donor's authorization form. It should be clear and easy for the donor, and easy for your staff to process. The service bureau and bank can provide these forms, but you will almost certainly be able to improve on them for your specific needs.

- Develop a marketing and PR plan to promote the program, define your strategy and offer, and detail the benefits to the donor.

- Develop your marketing materials. These can include brochures, telephone scripts, direct mail packages, newsletter copy, a posting for your Website or listserv, and anything else that comes to mind.

- Be careful *not* to assign your monthly giving program to a junior person who may not feel empowered to act. Junior people often don't swim, they tread water. If the development director is replaced, your monthly giving program may go into limbo.

Keep trying to convert donors to EFT

Promote EFT *constantly*—in special appeals, in renewal letters, in your prospect program, on the phone, and at special events.

Once you've launched the program, it's important to make your donors understand how cost-effective and convenient it is. A certain segment of your audience doesn't want to be the first to join something. But when they see something is successful and growing, with other people like themselves participating, they're far more willing to consider joining. This will be an important selling point, as your program develops.

Finally, stay in touch with your donors: Survey them periodically to find out what they want and whether they're happy. Discover how you can serve their interests better to keep them giving.

Case Study: Salvation Army, Tampa, Florida

Paul Kralovanec reports in *The Salvation Army On the Frontlines of Financial Development* (Vol. II, No.12) that their Hillsborough County Area command (Tampa) has had great success with EFT. When the command offered its monthly Bed & Bread Club members the opportunity to give by EFT, it discovered that more than 97 percent of pledges were fulfilled, in comparison with just 74 percent of check pledges. The annual renewal rate was 92 percent, compared to just 55 percent of non-EFT donors.

They have also found that their EFT donors still give to other direct mail appeals throughout the year.

"EFT donors are also ripe for personalized solicitations that may lead to planned gifts." Kralovanec says. "Remember, they already trust our organization enough to give us their bank account number."

That's my experience, too. These donors are saying they really care about you.

Credit cards: your second-best choice

As a rule, I prefer donors to give by EFT rather than credit card because they tend to give for more years and therefore generate greater net income. However, there are exceptions to that rule.

	Average Monthly Fulfillment
EFT	98% - 99.5%
Credit Card	93% - 97%

My friend Wendy Boyd managed Oxfam-Canada's monthly donor program for a number of years. One day she received a call from an EFT donor. She recognized the donor's name immediately for two reasons. First, he was giving $150 a month via EFT, and, second, in the preceding six months, two of his payments had been denied by the bank, which was quite rare.

The donor was phoning to apologize for the second bounced payment. He explained that he had a problem keeping enough funds in his account. And he said that while he was still very committed to Oxfam, in order to correct the problem he'd have to change his giving. And since he was pledging $1,800 a year, Wendy was more than a little dismayed.

Then he surprised her by saying, "Since I can't seem to keep enough money in my account, I'd like to change my $150 EFT gift to a $1,000 a month credit card gift."

In addition to having a happy ending, this tale indicates that nonprofits can recruit fairly high-dollar donors into monthly giving programs. If a method is convenient, and if the donor feels comfortable about it, then you'll profit handsomely.

Keep credit card costs in mind, however. For example, a $100 EFT gift may entail a fee of $0.50. By contrast, that same $100 gift transferred by credit card could generate the following charges:

> Base fee: $0.35
>
> Bank transaction fee: 0 to $.015
>
> Bank discount rate @ 2.66% or $2.66
>
> TOTAL: $3.16

Some advantages of credit card programs

Barbara Broome wanted to get a free airline ticket, so she decided to make her monthly pledge to a charity through her credit card. Her decision to give by credit card rather than by check meant that she never missed a payment. And, because her credit card company gave her a frequent-flyer point for each dollar spent, she felt she was getting a personal benefit as well.

In fact, she switched all her single-gift donations to her credit card as well.

The advantages of credit cards over billing statements are numerous. Donors tend to give for more years, and their fulfillment rate is close to 100 percent, as compared with a 60 to 90 percent fulfillment rate for billing statements. The combination of these factors means you make a lot more money over the lifetime of a credit card donor.

Another advantage is that once a monthly credit card donor joins a program, it's still more difficult for them to cancel than a donor who receives a monthly billing statement. There are just two ways for a donor to cancel a monthly credit card payment: either let the pledge lapse when the credit card expires or take the initiative to contact you. And for a donor to write or call you requires both action and time. With monthly billing, however, the "action" burden falls on the nonprofit. The donor may simply ignore the reminder bills you send.

Another potential benefit of credit card giving is that some nonprofits have discovered that these donors give larger monthly gifts than monthly statement members and even EFT members. And since their fulfillment rate is high, they must be cherished.

Many donors feel more comfortable with credit cards than with EFT. And despite numerous telemarketing scams, they're willing to give credit card numbers over the phone or by mail.

When people are on a monthly credit card donation plan, they can be called and successfully solicited for an additional special, one-time gift, without having to get a new authorization.

Maintaining credit card donors

A question I'm often asked is, "What percentage of a file that signs up on a credit card will continue giving?" In other words, "How many donors am I going to have after years of developing this type of program?"

This question is impossible to answer without analyzing your particular donor base, the quality of your program, how you promote it, how much you invest in promotion, and the other options you offer your donors. But, as a general rule, 80 to 90 percent will remain in the program after Year One, and a full 50 percent at the end of five years.

However, all credit cards have a built-in problem: The majority will expire within two years of the date a donor signs up. If, for example, a donor signs up in April of any given year and her credit card expires in August of the same year, then you must renew that donor only four months after she joined your program. Note: With U.S. banks aggressively selling new credit cards, they're bringing in less qualified cardholders. They often mitigate some of the risk by allowing only one year until expiration.

Take heart, though. You can easily plan for this renewal. On joining, the donor must provide you with his card's expiration date. This means you'll need to set up a system to contact people whose cards are about to expire.

Generally, you must time your renewal solicitation for approximately four weeks before an expiration date. That's because credit card companies tend to send out new cards about a month before their expiration date.

In planning your renewal strategy, you'll want to consider the effectiveness of mail versus phone solicitation. If you try to renew a donor by mail, it will be on the donor's initiative to respond. Typically, fewer than 30 percent do so. With some donors, you'll likely have to send a few letters. If you try to renew them by phone, it's an easy opportunity for them to cancel or reduce their gift. However, both methods present opportunities to upgrade your donors.

Consider how best to use each medium to motivate your donors to take action. Generally, the success rate for renewing monthly gifts is far greater over the phone and is very cost-effective. Telephoning also allows you to ensure that a donor won't miss any month's gift. But test sending a letter first: Direct mail still works quite well, and it's cheaper.

In the end, renewing credit card donations will inevitably result in the loss of a certain percentage of donors. So do your best to have a timely, effective renewal strategy to minimize the attrition.

Too many nonprofits falsify expiration dates by adding a year at expiration time so the gifts will continue. Although most credit card companies don't check expiration dates, this practice is illegal, a violation of ethics, and—need I add?—stupid. Don't even think about doing it!

Another challenge with credit cards is that people often lose, cancel, or change their cards without notifying you. People change cards to take advantage of better interest rates, lower fees, frequent flyer points, or other benefits. When this happens, you risk losing your donor. At the very least, a new card transfer will cost your organization some time and money.

Remember: Donors don't change banks (unless they move some distance from the bank), but they often change credit cards.

Convert credit card donors to EFT

From your organization's perspective (as well as the donor's), EFT is the most advantageous payment method. EFT donors are more loyal, so their Long-Term Value is greater and they reduce your workload and expenses as well. That's why it's advisable to maintain a continuing effort to convert credit card donors to EFT.

A strong, persuasive letter mailed three to six months after a donor signs up for a monthly credit card gift may be sufficient to convert her to EFT. The chances increase if you promote conversion to EFT on an ongoing basis—through letters a couple of times a year, and in your newsletters and other correspondence.

There's another, less obvious advantage of EFT over credit card giving: When a credit card transaction is rejected, you'll receive less information than you do when an EFT is rejected. The more information you have, the easier it is to re-start a donor's gifts!

When a donor enters her credit card number on a form, she may give you the wrong number. Or a staff person may mistake a "1" for a "7." In fact, you may get a lot of invalid account numbers. I suggest you call new monthly donors to thank them for joining and verify the credit card number over the phone.

In tens of thousands of credit card transactions in a recent year, CHI's Bob Wesolowski found an overall rejection rate of a whopping 12.3 percent. This varied from one organization to another, with fewer rejections in longer-running programs and at higher-dollar giving levels.

Nearly all the 12.3 percent rejects were accounted for as follows:

- declined - 7.1%

- lost, stolen, or on a credit card "watch" list - 3.9%

- invalid credit card number or expiration date - 1.3%

  (Note: "Declined" may mean the nonprofit has erroneously or lazily kept a former monthly donor on the active file!)

There were higher declines around holidays, in December, and during summer vacations. Often people rejoined two months later.

Grassroots groups like food banks tend to have higher rates of declines.

Credit card cancellations and refusals also vary by geographic area. Urban centers that aren't doing well economically will have higher cancellation rates. Suburbs generally suffer less in a slow economy and therefore produce fewer cancellations. People in more affluent postal or zip codes have fewer cancellations, as do higher-dollar donors.

What does a credit card program cost you?

A number of costs are associated with credit card donations. Here, for example, are those charged by one of North America's largest banks:

- $25 to set up the program

- $42.50 each month (plus tax) for the use of an authorization terminal

- a two percent service charge on all Visa transactions

- an additional eight-cent charge on all MasterCard and American Express transactions. (Many banks charge more.)

In addition to these measurable and predictable service fees, there are the commission rates charged by financial institutions. Some charge as little as two percent of the gift amount, others as high as seven percent!

One of my clients surveyed a number of banks to find the lowest rate, signing up with the one that offered the best deal. Ten months later, the bank tried to increase its charges, more than doubling the percentage it initially charged. Take this as a warning: If you negotiate a special deal with a bank, make sure you negotiate a *multi-year contract*.

Ninety to 95 percent of credit card transactions involve Visa or MasterCard, but American Express is trying to recruit nonprofit business, too. Because a donor may have any one of a number of reasons to favor using one card rather than another, many charities find it highly advantageous to offer American Express as a payment option.

Normally, Visa and MasterCard transactions require two days, meaning that if a deduction from a donor's account occurs on Tuesday, your organization will be credited for the transfer on Thursday. American Express offers a variety of choice of 1-day to 30-day transfers. (The percentage American Express deducts varies according to how long you let them keep your money. Naturally, they charge you more to send it quickly, and American Express' discount rate is typically much higher than MasterCard's or Visa's.)

Another problem with credit card commissions is that, while the percentage may be fixed, the dollar value increases as your donations increase.

If, for example, you're charged four percent for a credit card gift, you pay $0.40 on a $10.00 donation. However four percent of a $50-a-month gift is $2 per transaction, far greater than the $0.40 to $0.50 per gift you might pay with EFT. As you upgrade your donors, you'll pay the credit card company more money for the same amount of work.

There's a second variable cost that's often significant: the time it takes you to process each gift. Some smaller charities phone the credit card centers to clear each transaction. They're often put on hold and when their calls are taken, they can only clear a limited number of cards. That means making additional calls to the authorization centers—a waste of both time and money. These costs are not often properly calculated by charities.

To determine the cost of a staff person's time, calculate how many minutes (or even seconds) it takes that person to process a credit card transaction. Remember, the gross hourly wage should include benefits and holidays as well as salary. Add 40 percent to this estimate for other costs: office furniture, computer, office space, phones, etc. When all is said and done, a

$10-an-hour employee may easily cost you $20.

In addition, if it takes a staff person five minutes to process a $10 donation, you're not making much of a profit from the gift—even if you don't factor in your acquisition costs. (As a general principle, you should apply a similar calculation to all your fundraising programs.)

The final time-cost consideration is what I call the "opportunity cost factor." If your only fundraiser spends two months a year processing credit card gifts, then she is probably losing valuable time that could be devoted to more profitable areas, such as major gifts and planned giving.

When you consider all the costs related to processing each credit card transaction, you may decide to stop calling the credit card center to authorize each transaction. Better yet, you may simply lease or purchase an electronic point-of-sale terminal (a machine that automatically authorizes transactions for you). These machines, which you see almost every time you use a credit card, will save you time and money. However, their cost varies considerably, and you have to balance the cost against the volume of transactions you process (or anticipate processing).

One charity that decided not to authorize each gift received very few rejections, saving a phenomenal amount of staff and volunteer time. Virtually no one would intentionally give a nonprofit a credit card gift that was invalid. And since the vast majority of monthly gifts are between $10 and $25, you're at little risk of having a transaction denied. But check with your bank to find out their policy on not clearing transactions.

While it's worthwhile to clear gifts of $100 or more, it's logical to assume that most donors will have no problem clearing a modest transaction each month. Unless your credit card company tells you differently, and you believe them, I would assume you can process the gifts and deal with the small numbers of rejections after the fact. But calculate any time this could cost you, and factor it into your cost-benefit analysis.

Often the rejections you incur will be made up by the donors. And, just in case you wondered, people who steal credit cards are not likely to make gifts with the pilfered card!

Nonetheless, I do recommend you authorize a donor's first gift and the gifts of individuals with a track record of credit card transaction problems. In the case of the former, you'll occasionally make an error transcribing the account number, so it's worthwhile to verify it in a preliminary authorization. From then on, despite occasional problems, you'll make more money by saving the staff unnecessary time clearing each gift. Your staff will be much happier—this can be boring and frustrating work—and they'll devote the time they save to serving your donors in more fruitful ways.

Charge-backs

Charge-backs are another possible credit card cost. A charge-back occurs, for example, when a donor pledges to her local telethon, then sobers up and calls the credit card issuer to cancel the transaction. All she needs to say is that she didn't mean it. The nonprofit can be billed $10 to $25 for a charge-back.

When a nonprofit gets notice of a charge-back, the bank often just provides a credit card number, and not a donor's name. This can waste you a lot of time tracking who the donor is, since most organizations do not keep credit card information in a donor's database record. You can keep a separate file with numbers in numerical order as a cross-check.

If a donor causes you to incur a charge-back, that's an opportunity to ask that she switch to EFT. Ten to 40 percent of donors will comply under these circumstances, depending on how current and lengthy their giving is, how you ask them, and how good your program is.

Rules for authorization

You can take a single-gift credit card donation without a signed authorization—as a phone pledge, for example. But to withdraw a monthly gift by credit card, just as with EFT, you need written authorization. This is a legal requirement.

You must obtain and keep on file a signed, written agreement with the cardholder for all pre-authorized orders and recurring payments. This need not be in any specific form, but it must contain all the information necessary for processing the sales draft: card number, expiration date, cardholder's name, etc. The agreement must also include the amount to be charged to the cardholder's account, the frequency of the charge, and how long the charges will continue to be made.

Pre-authorized agreements must be made available to the bank upon demand. Authorized transactions may still be subject to charge-back.

When you ask your donor to give you credit-card information, you should word your form so you don't have to get a new authorization every time a card changes. For example, "I permit [*name of your organization*] to use updated credit card information that I provide from time to time." This allows you to obtain updated credit card information over the phone without having to get a signature. It's a good idea, as it will reduce maintenance costs and minimize the number of drop-offs.

What percentage of a donor file will give by credit card?

If you only offer your donors two choices—billing statements and credit cards—then more will opt for billing statements than for credit cards in your first year of operation. However, over time, you'll find a lower drop-off rate with credit card donors and a higher drop-off rate with monthly statement donors. And if you consistently promote electronic giving to your donors, you'll convert billing statement donors into credit card donors as time goes by, so the percentage on credit cards will grow each year.

If you only offer donors the EFT and credit card options, you'll likely attract more donors to EFT than to credit cards in most countries except, perhaps, the U.S. Since credit card donors have a slightly higher drop-off rate than EFT donors, it's in your best interest to try to promote EFT as the first and best choice, and also to convert credit card donors to EFT.

If you offer all three options—monthly billing, EFT, and credit card giving—the breakdown of people in each system will depend on many factors. That said, here's a summary of the ranges for clients with the various giving combinations (based on programs that have been active for five years or more).

Typical donor preferences, by method of payment

	Low end	High end
Between these two choices . . .		
EFT	60%	90%
Credit card	10%	40%
Between these two choices . . .		
Billing statement	50%	80%
Credit card	20%	50%
Among three choices . . . *		
EFT	25%	60%
Credit card	20%	50%
Billing statement	10%	50%

* Note: given the possible range, these don't add up to 100%

Socioeconomic factors may cause variations in preferences in payment options. For example, gay and lesbian groups tend to prefer credit cards by 3:1 to as much as 5:1. Groups like Common Cause and Public Citizen have used EFT and credit cards in equal amounts. Religious organizations and more traditional groups prefer EFT by 2:1.

Here's the situation at a "typical" U.S. client with a program that started only recently:

Twenty-five percent of the donors pay by credit card. Another 25 percent use EFT, while 50 percent are on a monthly billing system. Three years ago, combined electronic giving (EFT and credit card) was only 20 percent of the organization's file. Three years from now, that proportion will be 65-70 percent.

CHAPTER 8
Recruiting monthly donors by mail

Typically, direct mail is the centerpiece of a monthly donor recruitment program. Even if the telephone, television, or word-of-mouth is your primary vehicle to attract monthly givers, chances are you'll frequently communicate with both prospective and current monthly donors through the mail. Every time you mail something to one of your donors, you have an opportunity to promote your monthly giving program. The opportunities include:

- mention in annual and special appeals
- a sign-up section on your membership or donor acquisition reply form
- a reply form box "for more information" about monthly giving
- an invitation in a thank-you package
- wallet-flap envelopes (with a sign-up form on the perforated, extra-large flap that can be removed and inserted into the envelope)

For example, a direct mail monthly giving invitation package is usually best formatted as a closed-face, personalized letter with a commemorative stamp or two on the outer envelope. When you create a monthly giving program, make it look exclusive. You want donors to feel they're making significant contributions—that they're joining a special team that provides leadership to your cause.

When you're deciding what direct mail format to use, consider the following:

- Does this package make your offer look important, exclusive, and appealing?
- Do all of the elements work together: outer envelope, letter, reply form, reply envelope, and any other enclosures?
- Is your response form readable and attractive?

Dear Special Friend of NRDC,

The dictionary defines a "resource" as something that can be turned to for support or help.

At NRDC, our job is to defend natural resources like clean water, fresh air and wilderness lands from those who would despoil them for private gain.

But to do so, we depend on a "resource" of our own:

You.

You and your 170,000 fellow members nationwide not only provide us with a source of revenue to wage our legal battles -- you also make up a constituency that gives us both standing in court and influence in Congress. Without the "resource" you help comprise, NRDC simply couldn't survive.

And because of the staunch commitment you have made to our environmental work, I'd now like to offer you a unique opportunity to enhance the impact of your support for NRDC!

At NRDC, we are fortunate and grateful that we have a very small but dedicated group of members who have chosen to contribute to NRDC on an ongoing and predictable basis. These select members are part of a special committee called "Earth Advocates."

Earth Advocates have agreed to pledge a small amount of money each month in order to provide NRDC with a steady and reliable source of income. A source of income that not only enables us to respond quickly to emergencies, but that also allows us to take on projects that may require many years of effort.

Earth Advocates are truly a distinctive corps of our members. In fact, they make up less than one-half of one percent of our total membership.

Their impact on NRDC, however, is both enormous and invaluable. And I believe you would be an extraordinary addition to their ranks.

That's why I'm inviting you to become an Earth Advocate today. Because it is the single best way for you to enhance

(over, please)

40 West 20th Street • New York, NY 10011

d Paper

- 2 -

and extend the impact of your membership in NRDC.

Why are the Earth Advocates so important to us?

For three reasons:

FIRST, EARTH ADVOCATES ENABLE US TO MOVE QUICKLY.

When there is a massive oil spill in Alaska. When logging interests aggressively seek Congressional approval to allow commercial exploitation of yet another national forest. When a common pesticide has been discovered to be a dangerous carcinogen ... NRDC cannot afford to wait for financial support to materialize. We have to jump into battle immediately.

The Earth Advocates provide us with a war chest that can be used whenever and wherever it's needed. This dependable source of revenue means we can begin working on an environmental crisis within days -- sometimes hours -- of when it occurs.

SECOND, EARTH ADVOCATES ENABLE US TO TAKE ON LONG-TERM PROJECTS.

One of the cruel ironies of environmental work is that while disasters can take place in an instant (the Exxon Valdez, for example), the solutions to such problems may take many years.

Before NRDC can become involved in a long-term project, like protecting the tropical rainforests or reducing the use of ozone-depleting chemicals, we need to know we can see the project through to a successful conclusion.

In many cases our opponents know that our financial and human resources are stretched to the limit. They try to wear us down with delaying tactics and unnecessary paperwork.

But again, it's the Earth Advocates who come to the rescue. Their steady monthly support means that we can take on a case even if we know it will take five or ten years to win.

THIRD, EARTH ADVOCATES ALLOW US TO TACKLE A BROAD RANGE OF ISSUES.

Global warming, deforestation, water pollution, toxic waste, endangered species, pesticides ... many of these issues are related. In fact, few environmental problems are

(next page, please)

A monthly giving club invitation
letter *(this page and next)*
Illustration 8.1

isolated -- most are interconnected.

NRDC is one of the few environmental organizations that works across-the-board on <u>all</u> of these issues, and that's one reason why we're so effective. But there is a price to pay for this broad commitment: We are forced to keep many balls in the air at the same time, sometimes fighting dozens of legal battles simultaneously.

Here again, it's the Earth Advocates who make it all possible. Without their steady support, we would be forced to "rob Peter to pay Paul," taking funds away from one vital case to meet the needs of another. Thanks to the Earth Advocates, however, we have managed to remain at the center of virtually every major environmental issue facing our planet.

When you become an Earth Advocate by giving $15 or $20 a month to NRDC, your contribution will be used to pay all of the routine -- but utterly essential -- costs of carrying on our work in the courts, the media and the halls of government. Your $15 monthly contribution, for example, might be used to help ...

... pay for transcribing the deposition of a scientist in a federal case against a corporation polluting a river or bay;

... defray the costs of bringing an expert to testify before Congress on the catastrophic dangers of ozone depletion;

... pay for printing a Citizen Action Guide to help consumers avoid purchasing products that harm the environment;

... fund a grassroots citizens campaign to win worldwide protections like a Global Warming Treaty and rainforest preservation; or,

... pay the court costs of filing a lawsuit against a timber company's plan to clearcut a national forest.

Please remember that the <u>size</u> of your contribution is not as important as the regularity of it. Even 10 or 12 dollars can have an enormous impact on our work when it arrives in dependable monthly installments.

Stop and think about it. Ten or 12 dollars is what you pay to top off the gas in your car's tank. And you probably

(over, please)

have to do that at least once a week.

I'm asking you to spend the same amount <u>once a month</u> to help clean up our environment for yourself and your children.

But I don't want to minimize the importance of your sacrifice. In fact, I'm keenly aware that membership in Earth Advocates is a significant financial commitment for many NRDC members. But that also says something about the <u>depth</u> of their commitment.

Of course, you may cancel your membership in the Earth Advocates -- or change the size of your monthly pledge -- at any time, simply by notifying us. But I suspect that after you've had a chance to see the impact of your membership in this program, you'll want to stay on board for a long time.

Each month, I will send you our <u>Earth Advocates Update</u>. This newsletter -- exclusive to Earth Advocates -- will keep you informed on the progress of our work as well as to report on how your gift is being used.

As a member of NRDC, you are already a valuable "resource" in the struggle to save our environment.

But I'm asking you to become a renewable resource by joining the Earth Advocates today.

Please let me hear of your decision -- one way or the other -- by return mail.

Sincerely,

John

John H. Adams
Executive Director

P.S. As a member of the Earth Advocates, you will continue to enjoy all the benefits and privileges of membership in NRDC, including your subscription to the <u>Amicus Journal/NRDC Newsline</u>. However, you will no longer receive additional fundraising appeals for NRDC programs.

P.P.S. For a glimpse of how your membership in the Earth Advocates will affect our work, please read the enclosed note from David Doniger, one of our senior staff attorneys.

- Do you explain EFT, if this is a giving option?
- Are all the giving options clear?
- Is it clear what you're asking the donor to do?
- Do you restate your offer on the reply form, and will it compel a donor to take action immediately?

In any format test, you'll need to evaluate:
- the number of responses an appeal generates at a suggested pledge amount
- the percentage of responses an appeal generates at a suggested pledge amount
- average gift sizes
- the cost to recruit a new donor
- the cost of the appeal and the projected long-term income (varies by method of payment)

Let's assume the donor segments for this test were similar and the only test variable was the monthly gift request. Let's also assume the donors gave by EFT at the amount requested. We can examine the following figures to compare the levels of profitability at each Ask level tested.

# Mailed	Average Amount	# Responses	% Response	Ask Gift	1-Year Total	Total 1-year value
10M	$ 5	230	2.3%	$ 5	$ 60	$13,800
10M	$10	140	1.4%	$10	$120	$16,800
10M	$12	100	1.0%	$12	$144	$14,400
10M	$15	80	0.8%	$15	$180	$14,400
10M	$20	50	0.5%	$20	$240	$12,000

In this example, the most successful Ask is $10/month. It produced more gross income. Even factoring in the cost of servicing a larger number of $10/month donors than those at $12 or $15/month, net income will be higher.

The $12 and $15 Asks pull in equal amounts. But it costs a little more to service 100 donors (at $12/month) than 80 people (at $15). On the other hand, the more people in the program, the more potential you have for upgrading them. Also, the larger your program, the lower the per-unit cost for communication. You'll have to decide whether, given equal income, you prefer a higher average gift or more donors.

The best way to segment your file into test groups is by similar characteristics. Examples include:

- new donors
- multi-year donors
- donors at different giving levels
- recency
- frequency
- size of most recent gift
- gender
- years as a donor
- total giving
- volunteers
- donors who have come from a certain type of list
- donors who came from a particular channel (direct mail, phone, Web)
- members

The best segments to convert—usually

You can categorize your donor list in many different ways. The most important criteria for selection are usually gift size, recency, and multi-donors.

Generally, the best segments of your list for conversion to monthly donors will be active multi-donors, but new donors can also be considered hot prospects. Examining a donor's years of giving can also indicate their commitment, and their potential for making a monthly pledge.

Another excellent segment is lapsed monthly donors. People lapse for good reasons such as losing a job, irritation at a particular organizational policy, etc. But, one year later, their circumstances may have completely changed. They've already proven they are willing to make a monthly commitment, and you can renew them at a very cost-effective level. But make sure you record the reasons they drop out.

It's important to keep track of the original source of a donor, both by recruitment channel and by list, because both will affect Long-Term Value. And tracking these two sources are more important in your monthly giving program than anywhere else.

You are invited to become a charter member of MAP International's

Healing
PARTNERS

This select group of men and women commits to send a gift each month to help MAP provide lifesaving medicines and medical supplies to the world's neediest people. The amount of your monthly gift is between you and the Lord.

Knowing that funds will be there when needed enables MAP to respond quickly to severe medical emergencies while meeting our ongoing commitments to struggling hospitals and health clinics.

Your charter membership also entitles you to receive:

◆ **Special books and resource materials**

◆ **Quarterly field reports**

◆ *MAP International Report*

◆ **Regular communication from MAP president and CEO Paul Thompson, briefing you on critical MAP projects**

"As the person responsible for generating the resources MAP needs to serve the world's neediest people, I am very excited about our Healing Partners. And I want to encourage you to take advantage of this opportunity to become a charter member."

Larry Dixon, Vice Chairman
MAP Board of Directors

An insert with a monthly giving invitation letter
Illustration 8.2

In my experience, donors acquired from cause-related organizations have generally yielded a higher percentage of monthly givers. So donors from these lists may prove to be better long-term investments for you.

Here is an example of what a nonprofit organization, pulling an average return of one percent, might expect from a prospect mailing in which cause-related lists were used:

		Number Mailed	Number of Gifts	Average $ Amt. Gift
List A	Environmental	10,000	90	$25
List B	International Aid	10,000	100	$24
List C	Health	10,000	200	$24
List D	Religious	10,000	130	$16

In this prospect mailing example, the income per thousand for the International Aid list is 50 percent less than that of the Health list. But once on your house file, you may well find that many more donors from the International Aid list convert to monthly giving. This is because they are conditioned to the concept, as International Aid organizations are far more likely to have monthly giving clubs than the average nonprofit.

If you convert 20 percent of the International Aid donors to a monthly program and only 5 percent of the Health charity donors, you will find the former list to have much greater value over time. You'll see that some lists may double in value if you just calculate the yearly income from monthly donors.

What's worked for me

It's hard to generalize about what works, because every organization's list is unique. Here, though, are some elements I've tested that seem to pay off for most organizations:

- Offers with premiums tend to pull in more monthly donors, making premiums cost-effective.

- Giving a premium for joining at a higher entry-level increases the average gift per month.

- Donors who make several gifts a year are more likely to become monthly donors than those who give once a year, regardless of gift size.

- Personalization pays off in invitation letters.

- Using live stamps on reply envelopes increases response rates and is cost-effective.

- A subtle Ask for a monthly pledge in a prospect mail package pays off, so long as it isn't the primary focus of the appeal.

- People who drop out of a program are highly renewable.

- Lapsing donors who mail a monthly check need to be contacted soon after their checks stop coming, preferably by phone. Their re-entry into the program is directly related to how long you wait to call them. The sooner, the better.

- Lapsing EFT donors are best renewed by paying attention to why they lapsed; they usually volunteer a reason why they quit. If they drop out because they lost a job, go back to them in six or nine or twelve months. The best time to re-approach them depends on why they lapsed, but many tests show this is a very good segment.

We cordially invite

Mr. A. J. Smith

to become an honored member
of the

BIBLE-A-MONTH CLUB

with all privileges and blessings that
membership in this circle of caring
friends confers.

Insert in a monthly giving invitation package
Illustration 8.3

As a Bible-a-Month Club member you will receive:

A free subscription to the *American Bible Society Record*, the monthly magazine that shows you the difference your gifts are making in individual lives and in entire countries.

A colorful wall map to help you identify the places where your Bible-a-Month Club gifts are providing Bibles.

Monthly updates will let you know where your Bible-a-Month Club gifts are being used. You will also get a sample verse in one of the languages spoken by the people who will receive your gift Bibles.

A membership card that identifies you as a part of this Bible-sharing fellowship. Keep it with you as a reminder of your valued participation.

Bible-a-Month Club® • American Bible Society • 1865 Broadway • New York, NY 10023-7505

An insert that dramatizes the benefits of monthly giving
Illustration 8.4

An important word of caution about these lessons I've learned from testing: For some nonprofits, the opposite will be true. For instance, live stamps may decrease the response rate to an invitation package, or they may make the package less cost-effective. Be careful to test what's important. Your donors may not react like supporters of other causes.

Always keep in mind your donors' Long-Term Value. A certain list (or segment) may not do especially well in a specific test mailing, but you may find the monthly donors you recruit from this list give more money for more years than a list that seemed to "win" in an initial mailing. Tracking your donor patterns and giving behavior over time is the only way to determine Long-Term Value.

Many nonprofits only track their mail results for 65 to 90 days. However, this may not be long enough. This is especially true with large mailings, because results can trickle in for a year and a winning package can lose over that time. Short-term tracking can also disguise Long-Term Value. In fact, the focus on short-term results can ultimately have disastrous consequences. Consider this example:

- A religious mailer gets the following results from a 200,000-piece test of two direct mail prospect packages, with each package mailed to 100,000 addresses. Package A pulls in 1,000 donors and gross revenue of $22,000, for an average gift of $22. Package B pulls $18,000 from 900 donors, or $20 each.

- Looking at this single mailing, Package A out-pulls B both in the number of new gifts and the average gift size. It earns 22 cents per piece, compared to 18 cents per piece for Package B. This means

Short-Term View
200 M Piece Mailing

	Package A respondents	Package B respondents
Number mailed	100,000	100,000
Gifts	1,000	900
Percentage response	1%	0.9%
Average gift	$22	$20
Gross revenue	$22,000	$18,000
Income per piece	**$0.22**	**$0.18**

Package A pulls in $.04 more per piece or 22% higher income per piece—very signficant.

Long-Term View
5 years of returns from these donors

	Package A respondents 1000 donors	Package B respondents 900 donors
Total additional gifts	1,410	1,740
Average gift	$24.10	$25.40
Gross Income	$33,981	$44,196
Number of monthly donors	40	80
Number of gifts over 5 years	1,600	3,240
Average gift	$10	$10
Monthly income	$16,000	$32,400
5-year Gross	**$49,981**	**$76,596**

Over the long term, the B package-acquired donors produce much more money.

Yes, I want to take advantage of the convenience of Bread for the World's AUTOGIVE program and authorize my bank to begin monthly contributions to:

☐ Bread for the World
☐ Bread for the World Institute on Hunger & Development

Enclosed is my *first monthly contribution* of:
☐ **$15** ☐ **$30** ☐ **$40** (Full Harvest Member) ☐ $ _____

I would like my gift processed each month on the ☐ 5th ☐ 20th

My signature _____ Date _____

☐ I prefer to make a *special gift* of $ _____ since I'm unable to make a monthly commitment at this time.

Mr. John Doe
123 Any Street
Any Town, AS 00000

95DOE
0000000
See reverse side for important information. ▶ ▶

▲ *Please detach here and return top portion with your check. Thank you.*

When you use the convenience of Bread for the World's AUTOGIVE program . . .

■ Your membership will be automatically renewed each year
■ You will receive an attractive Bread for the World lapel pin
■ Your Bread for the World newsletter will be mailed first class so you will receive information on critical legislation right away
■ You'll receive Bread for the World's ANNUAL REPORT, distributed on Capitol Hill and around the country
■ You'll be invited to national gatherings and other events in Washington, D.C., and around the country
■ A monthly record of your gifts will appear on your bank statement
■ Your gift is more effective because our administration and postage costs are lower

Remember: you may increase—or discontinue—your monthly contributions at any time.

Bread for the World
802 Rhode Island Avenue, N.E.
Washington, DC 20018
(202) 269-0200

RECYCLED PAPER 60052

Response device from a monthly giving invitation sent
to members a few months after a lump-sum gift
Illustration 8.5

that A pulled 22 percent more income per piece than B—a significant difference. It's the clear winner, and most nonprofits would re-use it as the control package for future mailings.

■ However, tracking these donors over time reveals that Package B respondents renew at a higher rate and are more likely to become monthly donors. Over time, their cumulative gifts will far exceed those of Package A.

If certain lists or segments seem to be marginal when you are recruiting monthly donors, try different portions of the list. For instance, I've succeeded in turning around a money-losing list by selecting certain members from it, such as those living in particular states or provinces, cities, or even areas of a city. Or I may choose prospects whose zip or postal codes match those already in the program or on my particular donor base. I may select males or females depending on the cause. I may select "hot-line" donors or buyers who have donated within the most recent 30-, 60-, or 90-day period. When possible, I'll often pay more for donors who give larger gifts because this is usually worthwhile.

When you test, be sure to test the big things—not trivial elements. Generally, this will mean testing:

- your medium (e.g., direct mail, telemarketing, or television) to compare the cost-effectiveness of one against another

- your copy platform or offer

- your format

- the time when you invite donors to join the program (for example, after they make their third gift in a year, only at the beginning of a year, etc.)

CHAPTER 9
Recruiting monthly donors by phone

As you may know, telemarketing is an effective way to persuade people to give. And if you've read this far, you know that each monthly donor you recruit is worth hundreds, possibly thousands, of dollars. So it's time to consider marrying those two lessons.

First, to clear the air of this often controversial topic of telemarketing, I confess: I personally hate receiving these calls. But I recognize the power of the medium, and I have to say (with some reluctance) that telemarketing has often proven to be the most cost-effective way to build monthly giving programs.

I've had greater success in recruiting monthly donors with a combination of direct mail and telephone invitations than with stand-alone telephone calls.

There are many ways the telephone can be used to build your monthly donor club:

- to recruit new monthly donors
- to upgrade current monthly donors
- to renew lapsed monthly donors
- to survey monthly pledgers
- to enhance your relationship with your monthly donors by building a personal connection and by giving them the information they want
- to get new expiration dates for credit cards about to self-destruct

Who are you going to call?

It's important to distinguish between two types of telemarketing: calling individuals from your donor list and making "cold calls" to people with no previous relationship with your organization. *I recommend calling only your donors.* For your house file donors, monthly donor recruitment over the phone can be very successful.

The amount you ask for should be related to each person's giving history. If you call a person who gives $100 three times per year (for a total annual donation of $300), ask her for an amount that would upgrade her annual giving. A reasonable range is $30 to $100 per month. Start high, then negotiate down.

You can break your list down into various segments: active donors, new donors, multi-gift donors, multi-year donors, lapsed donors, etc. These segments can be broken down further by gift amount, recency or frequency, sex, etc. It all depends on how much you know about your donors and the propensity of various donor segments to join a monthly giving program. Remember, it makes no sense for most organizations to phone a $3 donor to ask her to make a $10-a-month commitment: It's simply not cost-effective and won't work.

Multiple-gift donors may be your best bet, but single donors can still be highly profitable to convert. More recent donors and $20+ donors will outperform those who haven't given in a year, or who give under $20.

Generally, your recruitment efforts will be more successful when you phone the following groups:

- new donors
- recently renewed donors
- people who give more than one gift in a year
- people on your donor base for many years

For your monthly donor appeal, the segments that work well in the mail are the ones most likely to work well over the phone.

Once you have determined the kind of individuals you will target, you can tailor the telemarketing script for them. For example, multi-gift donors will usually need a slightly different message than new donors. First, you want to remind them that they've given a number of gifts over the year. You'll also want to tell them they're among your most committed donors, which is why they're being asked to join this special club.

For new donors, emphasize the special nature of the club. Explain that you're inviting them to join because of their recent generous commitment. And you believe that this is one of the best ways for them to continue their support.

Canadian telemarketing pro Bob Penner says that "In many cases, it's not a new script you need, but a well-trained and experienced caller, who knows how to nuance the pitch, based on the donor history they have in front of them. You can't script every possibility, although you can script for the major ones."

With good database management and donor research, you can create a profile of who these individuals are. Research and testing helps you find out how and why people react to your letters and phone calls. Based on this information, you can then create your strategy.

Usually, the success of your telephone program will be proportional to the success of your direct mail appeals. For example, if your first annual renewal mailing is your top grossing letter of the year, you will enjoy similar success with a phone campaign focused on your annual renewal.

Selecting the right offer

You must be very careful when selecting an offer for the telephone, since you won't have as much time to explain it as you would in a long letter. You are also trying to engage a prospect in conversation, so it has to be a clear Ask for a specific kind of work.

The key considerations are:

- what amount to ask for
- what premium to offer (if any)
- what product option to offer

Callers must try to learn what might motivate a donor to give you a monthly gift. If the donor shows a particular interest in a special project, that's what should be emphasized in the call.

You also have to decide what payment options you will offer. A credit card may be your best option for a telemarketing campaign, because the entire process can be done over the phone. However, these days many people are leery of giving out their credit card numbers, so you'll have to find out how sensitive your prospects are.

If you decide to recruit people for EFT, they will have to send you one of the following:

- a check made out for the monthly amount
- a check marked "void"
- their checks' "transit" or "routing" number

This complicates matters slightly. However, it can pay off to try this. You must immediately send the pledger a "thank you for your commitment" letter. Include their personalized pledge form and details of what they have to do, i.e., authorize the bank transfer and return a voided check in the postage-paid envelope. The authorization form should say something like: "I agree to have [*dollar amount*] deducted from my checking account on the [*date*] of each month."

The third payment option is by check. If the donors choose this option, you should immediately send them the "thank you for your commitment" pledge form and letter and ask them to return their first monthly check in your reply envelope. And you can use this opportunity to try to convert them to electronic giving.

Should you send a letter first?

I strongly recommend testing a pre-call letter (a letter that announces you will be calling the donor within a few days). In the letter, state your marketing proposition, the importance of their decision to give monthly, and its value to the cause they care so much about.

Then call within two weeks to invite them to join.

In your call, be as specific as possible about the reason they should make a monthly gift—to build a new day care center, to run a campaign, to pay off a hospice mortgage.

Follow-up materials

Before you start the actual calling campaign, you need to know what to do when a donor pledges, when a donor says No, and when you can't contact a donor. You also have to plan all your follow-up strategies and print the appropriate materials.

If donors pledge by credit card, ask them to give you their card number, the name as it appears on the card, and the expiration date. If they are willing to give by EFT, most will also give you the "transit number" at the bottom of their checks. Then you simply send them a confirmation letter that thanks them and asks them to notify you if there is an error, or if they've changed their mind. Give pledgers a date by which they need to respond before you make the first deduction. A couple of weeks is a good idea. Then, if you don't hear from them, their donations are transferred to your account monthly.

account. And it will be a <u>continuing</u> commitment --
from you and your fellow PARTNERS OF CONSCIENCE --
that will enable us to sustain and expand our
lifesaving work.

I've enclosed your first PARTNERS OF
CONSCIENCE reminder -- along with details of how
you may conveniently make your monthly contributions
automatically, should you wish to do so.

Again, thank you for reaching out to those who
depend on Amnesty members like you ... determined
to see justice and humanity in our lifetime and
unwilling to settle for less.

Sincerely,

Bill Schulz

William F. Schulz
Executive Director

Partners

OF CONSCIENCE

Dear Partner of Conscience:

I'm writing to say "thank you" -- not only for
your recent contribution to Amnesty, but for the
extraordinary commitment represented by your
decision to become a PARTNER OF CONSCIENCE.

It is only because of loyal members like you --
who understand the importance of regular, <u>dependable</u>
financial support to Amnesty's worldwide efforts on
behalf of human rights -- that our work can succeed.
And it <u>must</u> succeed.

Because in a chaotic post-Cold War world
racked by vicious and escalating human rights
emergencies -- met all too often by the blatant
inattention and inaction of world governments --
Amnesty must have the power to exert <u>more</u> citizen
pressure and the resources to take <u>more</u> effective
action, if we are ever to move forward into a
safer future.

Each day, we are horrified by tales of "ethnic
cleansing" in Bosnia, continued killings and
torture in Indonesia, Iran or Haiti, atrocities
against Shiites in Iraq, and unspeakable treatment
of prisoners and forced "confessions" from every
corner of the world.

Only a worldwide movement can succeed against
such outrages. And because governments don't take
a stand, Amnesty International must. It can only
begin with the commitment of <u>individuals</u>.

We depend on Amnesty members for that
commitment, and none more so than PARTNERS OF
CONSCIENCE like you.

It is your commitment and generosity that has
already helped free or better the situation of
thousands of prisoners and put the tyrants of the
world on notice that they, too, can be brought to

Amnesty International USA • 322 Eighth Avenue • New York, NY 10001

♻ RECYCLED PAPER

Portions of a thank-you to
a new monthly donor
Illustration 9.1

Partners
OF CONSCIENCE

Reminder Statement

John Doe
1357 Main Street, W.
Washington, DC 02020

Pledge due (see below) _____

Extra gift this month _____

00098544   SU4303
Please show any change in your name or address.

TOTAL ENCLOSED _____

Please return this portion of the statement with your check made payable to Amnesty International USA, P.O. Box 96756, Washington, D.C. 20090-6756. If your donation is greater than your pledge, please advise us if it is to be applied to future months or is an extra gift (complete box above). Contributions received after the 16th may not be posted until next month.

Pledge Amount: ___5.00___   Partner of Conscience Since: ___03/94___

Date Due	Amount Pledged	Status	Date Received	Amount Paid
03/16/94	5.00	PAID	03/04/94	5.00
04/16/94	5.00	OPEN		

SEE THE ENCLOSED INFORMATION ABOUT OUR AUTOMATIC PAYMENT PLAN.
THIS PLAN ALLOWS US TO PUT MORE RESOURCES INTO THE FIGHT FOR
HUMAN RIGHTS. SIGN UP TODAY!

This statement is a reminder of your voluntary agreement. Your tax-deductible pledge is helping Amnesty International expand its human rights actions throughout the world. Thank you for your generous support.

 Recycled Paper

A monthly giving reminder statement
Illustration 9.2

E-mail and fax can get forms to people instantly and may be worth testing. While immediate, these methods lack the more personal aspect of a thank-you letter and reply envelope.

As with other forms of phoning, 60 percent to 80 percent of current donors fulfill their pledge. Some people change their minds but will still send you a one-time gift.

When a donor pledges

When a donor pledges by phone, send a thank-you letter immediately—that same evening if possible, or the next day. For both EFT and monthly statement donors, your goal is to persuade each donor to send you a check. The best way to do that is to get their commitment forms and letters into their hands as soon as possible after the call. (In a local campaign, you could have volunteers pick up the donor's check and get their signature on the authorization form.)

You can enhance the response rate for this all-important first check, or voided check, by handwriting the individual caller's name, in blue ink, on the envelope, and on the signature line of the thank-you letter.

For credit card donors, send a prompt thank-you saying that you greatly appreciate their strong commitment to your cause and remind them that this amount of money will be deducted on the date they have selected.

When a donor receives your call, he can make a number of decisions:

- *To give:* to become a monthly donor; to try it for a few months; to send a single gift.

- *To postpone:* to talk to their spouse; to think about it; to ask you to call back at a better time.

- *To decline:* to tell you never to call again; to tell you never to contact them in any way again; to tell you they are not interested in helping as a monthly donor.

When a donor says No

A donor may say No in one of three ways:

- She could say she would *never* join a program, in which case her records should be tagged appropriately to save you money and to save her irritation by avoiding future invitations.

- She could say "No, *not at this time,*" in which case you may want to get back to her in the future (especially if she gives you a reason why she won't take part now).

- 2 -

launching an URGENT ACTION appeal -- <u>without</u> having to weaken our long-term program efforts.

I never want funding constraints to force me to make that kind of desperate trade-off. And it is because of our PARTNERS OF CONSCIENCE that we've been spared that painful choice.

When you become a PARTNER OF CONSCIENCE, I will send you a unique black-and-gold pin that will identify your special commitment to human rights.

You may have seen other Amnesty Members wearing this quiet symbol, and wondered what it meant. When I am asked this question myself, I tell people the story you can read in the accompanying letter from Maryam Elahi, an expert on the Middle East, who works in our Washington, D.C. office.

Maryam had a chance to see for herself the kind of hope this pin represents for those unjustly imprisoned and brutalized by governments the world over.

When you have read her letter and shared her experience of Amnesty in action, I hope you will act immediately to become a PARTNER OF CONSCIENCE.

Remember, <u>Amnesty International receives no funding of any kind from any government in the world</u> -- nor would we accept any and thus compromise our ability to act.

Instead, we rely on the concern and generosity of members like you, and especially on the small group of members who have become PARTNERS OF CONSCIENCE.

In a world where newly emerging governments and their people struggle to hold on to their fragile hope for freedom, it is also true that for many thousands of prisoners of conscience in other lands, very little has changed at all.

For far too many people, true deliverance is still a distant dream. <u>But I believe it is a dream that you and I can help make come true with our commitment and our determination</u>, just as we did not long ago in Morocco.

Please become a PARTNER OF CONSCIENCE today. Together, we can and will silence the screams and light the darkness.

Sincerely,

William F. Schulz
Executive Director

A letter mailed to a donor
who could not be
contacted by telephone
Illustration 9.3

---

ers

SCIENCE

ar Amnesty Member:

Recently, one of our telephone representatives tried o contact you -- without success, I'm afraid. The eason we called was to ask you to join those Amnesty embers who have taken their dedication to our struggle one step further by becoming a PARTNER OF CONSCIENCE.

The promise of new democracies has been tempered by the rise of old hatreds and new kinds of human rights abuses. Somalia and Bosnia remind us that the dark history of past holocausts can indeed be repeated. And as new victims replace old ones, the need for Amnesty's work is as urgent and profound as ever.

It's the regular monthly support of our PARTNERS OF CONSCIENCE who provide the income to enable Amnesty International to sustain the kind of long-range, tenacious effort that is often essential to freeing those men and women who have been consigned by their governments to virtual oblivion ... abandoned to die ... unseen and unremembered by the outside world. And these efforts would simply not be possible without a base of consistent, <u>predictable</u> income we can count on.

For example, we learned that years of persistent work on behalf of almost 300 "disappeared" prisoners held by Moroccan authorities had not been in vain.

<u>We had never given up</u> in our efforts to learn the fate and secure the release of these men and women. Upon their release, we learned that many had been held at the infamous Tazmamert secret detention center and other secret facilities, some for <u>more than 15 years past the end of their sentences</u>. Locked away in the dark. Never allowed out of their cells. Never treated for their wounds or illnesses. Some even permanently blinded by their barbaric ordeal in darkness.

Without the predictable base of support provided by our PARTNERS OF CONSCIENCE, it would be almost impossible to sustain the long-range commitment such efforts require.

And I'm afraid that the end result would be measured in the most painful terms possible: fewer prisoners of conscience released ... and an increase in both the brutal torture used to extract information from them or the killing meant to silence them forever.

Moreover, the dependable support provided by our PARTNERS OF CONSCIENCE also enables us to respond quickly to a breaking human rights crisis, when human lives depend on our ability to move <u>immediately</u> -- such as by

Amnesty International USA • 322 Eighth Avenue • New York, New York 10001

- She could say No but offer a *single gift*, in which case you send her a warm thank-you letter and subtly ask her to reconsider, enclosing the appropriate reply form so she can change her mind. This also gives you an opportunity to explain the program again in more detail: "Because we didn't want to tie up too much of your time, perhaps we didn't fully explain how advantageous this program is both to you and to our organization" (followed, of course, by many reasons why it would be great if she joined the club at this time).

When you can't make contact

You'll also find that there are many donors you cannot contact. If you consistently get an answering machine, the donor may be out of town or screening his calls. Consider tagging this file and coming back to it within a month. If you haven't reached a contact after several attempts, you can test a message on his answering machine and ask him to call you. This can produce results. Ideally, your caller leaves his name and a toll-free number.

Perhaps you never get through; maybe they get too many telemarketing calls, or they never answer their phone. In that case, it's probably a good idea to send them a letter, especially if they're in a segment that works well. You could say, "We tried to get hold of you by phone but were unable to." Or, "The reason we called you is because we've set up an important new club. And I wanted to invite you to become one of the first members."

What to do with hostile donors

Assuming the people you phone are good donors, you want to be very careful about offending them. If you get a hostile reaction, code angry donors with "never call" in your database. Send angry donors an apology and give them your private number and a time when they can call you to discuss how they felt about the telemarketing call. Again, you will learn something of value—and may save a donor relationship. You don't necessarily want to do this if you get a complaint from a one-time $5 donor. But, you certainly want to do it for a multi-year large gift donor.

Many nonprofits have discovered that donors who say No to a call are actually more, not less, likely to respond positively to the next appeal by mail.

How to follow up on a pledge not fulfilled

In all telemarketing campaigns, a certain percentage of people don't follow through on their commitments to give. It may be because they changed their minds, forgot to do it, or even lied to get the caller off the phone. This is also a problem in monthly donor phone recruitment. But when a donor commits by credit card, or reads his check transit or routing number to your caller, that dramatically increases pledge fulfillment.

Higher fulfillment levels are related to how soon people get their pledge commitment letter in the mail. If it arrives within 48 hours, the fulfillment rate can be 80 to 90 percent or more; if it arrives two weeks later, this could easily drop to 50 percent. It's crucial to get these letters out immediately.

When individuals don't send in their first check or a voided check, follow up on them as soon as possible. Do not wait any longer than two to four weeks, depending on how far the mail has to travel. Of course, how long it takes you to process pledges and organize a second call has an impact on how soon you get back to a person.

Ten days after the first reminder, if you still haven't received a check from them, give them another call. Ask if there was a misunderstanding or if it got into the mail late, and ask if they would like another reminder notice with a reply envelope.

Once they've made their commitment, send them another thank-you—a different thank-you—for fulfilling their commitment.

Who will run your program?

You have two choices on who will manage your program: (a) in-house staff or volunteers, or (b) an outside telemarketing firm.

Remember, in-house programs often fail. Like many forms of fundraising, telemarketing is more difficult and more expensive than people think. If you decide to do your program in-house, you must have:

- sufficient staff to manage the program
- enough resources to run the program
- enough phones
- easy access to your database for operators
- the ability to follow up
- the ability to recruit and train enough staff and volunteers
- the expertise to write proper scripts

- the phone numbers of your prospects
- an experienced phone canvass manager

I also suggest you ask yourself:

- Is your staff time better spent doing something else?
- Can you properly manage a program?
- How effective will your volunteers be if they're doing the calling, and can they be trained?
- How cost-effective are volunteers, compared with paid staff?
- If you decide to use paid staff, can you recruit a quality group?
- Have you compared the overall cost-benefit of using an outside telemarketing firm versus doing it in-house?

If you decide to do an in-house program, you should test your results against a professional telemarketing firm. You'll learn a lot from a professional firm and will find it much easier to bring it in-house on a later campaign, if you choose to do so.

It's critical to check out telemarketing firms carefully, because there are many ethically challenged telemarketing operations. These unscrupulous firms exploit some of the most vulnerable people in our society, and their actions discredit philanthropy. This makes it much more difficult for telemarketers with integrity (who are still in the majority) to do their jobs.

It's also important for you to track a telemarketing campaign on a daily basis, and it's crucial to know exactly what percentage of pledges are fulfilled over time. Money promised is great, but pledges fulfilled are what you're really interested in. For instance, if only 60 percent of your monthly pledgers are still giving after three months, that will have a great impact on your cost-benefit ratio.

You need to track the fulfillment levels for years, especially for monthly check donors. People donating by EFT or credit card have very high fulfillment rates. But check donors can drop off quickly, so you need to track these donors over the long run to know their Long-Term Value.

The seven big advantages of telemarketing

- higher response rates than mail
- instant feedback from donors
- instant analysis of effectiveness

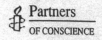

Partners
OF CONSCIENCE

Dear Amnesty Member:

I've just learned of the telephone conversation in which you have pledged to make a special contribution to Amnesty International. Please accept my sincere thanks.

The promise of new democracies has been tempered by the rise of old hatreds and new kinds of human rights abuses. Somalia and Bosnia remind us that the dark history of past holocausts can indeed be repeated. And as new victims replace old ones, the need for Amnesty's work is as urgent and profound as ever.

But in this age of historic transition, there is still a profound hope that a better world of human rights and personal dignity will emerge. And those of us who work to free prisoners of conscience are sustained in that hope by a thousand moments of individual courage and sacrifice.

Moments when men and women deliberately risk arrest, torture or execution to move one step closer to freedom. Or when people are simply swept up by a merciless and arbitrary state -- and must suddenly summon up the courage to deal with a level of horror and inhuman cruelty they may never have imagined.

As a member of Amnesty, you have come to know those moments of courage very well indeed. For it is your strong commitment and willing generosity that have enabled Amnesty International to become a light of hope for thousands of victims of human rights abuse all over the world.

For many of these men and women, Amnesty's candle of hope within a circle of barbed wire is far more than a mere symbol. It is the most real evidence of hope they have -- casting a light that reaches even into their dark and lonely cells with proof that they are not forgotten.

But these thousands of candles of hope only burn because of concerned citizens like you -- compassionate men and women who refuse to stand by and accept unjust

Amnesty International USA • 322 Eighth Avenue • New York, New York 10001

RECYCLED PAPER

A reminder letter to follow up a telephone pledge *(this page and next)*
Illustration 9.4

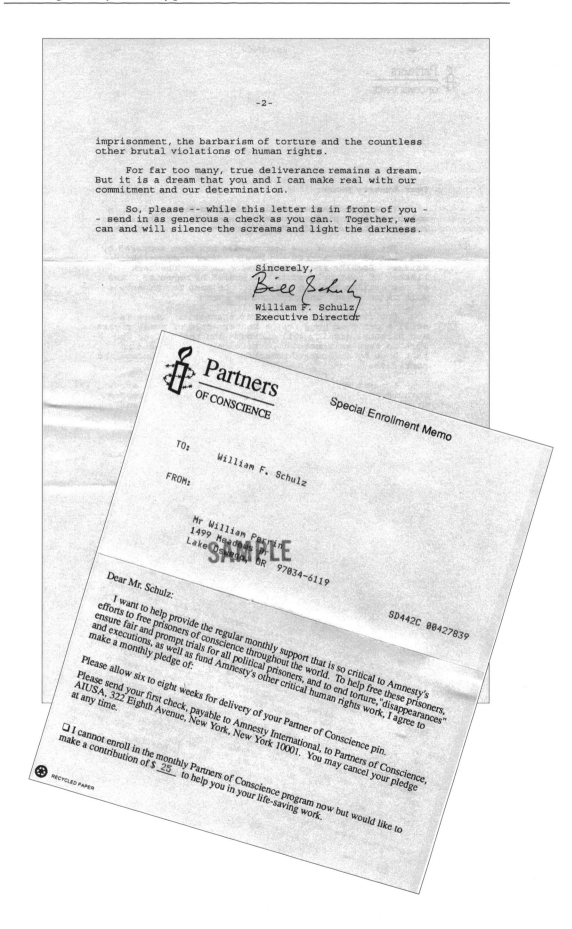

-2-

imprisonment, the barbarism of torture and the countless
other brutal violations of human rights.

    For far too many, true deliverance remains a dream.
But it is a dream that you and I can make real with our
commitment and our determination.

    So, please -- while this letter is in front of you -
- send in as generous a check as you can. Together, we
can and will silence the screams and light the darkness.

                              Sincerely,

                              William F. Schulz
                              Executive Director

Partners
OF CONSCIENCE   Special Enrollment Memo

TO: William F. Schulz

FROM:

           Mr William Pennin
           1499 Meadows Dr
           Lake Oswego, OR 97034-6119   SAMPLE

                                               SD442C 00427839

Dear Mr. Schulz:

    I want to help provide the regular monthly support that is so critical to Amnesty's
efforts to free prisoners of conscience throughout the world. To help free these prisoners,
ensure fair and prompt trials for all political prisoners, and to end torture, "disappearances"
and executions, as well as fund Amnesty's other critical human rights work, I agree to
make a monthly pledge of:

Please allow six to eight weeks for delivery of your Partner of Conscience pin.
Please send your first check, payable to Amnesty International, to Partners of Conscience,
AIUSA, 322 Eighth Avenue, New York, New York 10001. You may cancel your pledge
at any time.

☐ I cannot enroll in the monthly Partners of Conscience program now but would like to
make a contribution of $ __25__ to help you in your life-saving work.

♻ RECYCLED PAPER

- cost control—you can pull the plug if it's not working, double the callers if it is

- the possibility of negotiating a higher gift if you have a good caller

- single gifts may cover all the costs—the monthly donor pledges are all profit

- the ability to update errors in files

Keep in mind, however, that telemarketing also has two disadvantages. It's much more expensive than mail, and, like it or not, there are lots of people who detest telemarketing. If you start losing donors because of telemarketing, it can cost you a lot in the long run. (Some fundraisers believe that only a tiny percentage of donors resist telemarketing, but I've done enough radio phone-in shows on fundraising, spoken to enough large audiences of fundraisers, and seen enough surveys, to believe the numbers are significant.)

There are many other uses for telemarketing:

- You can use the telephone to strengthen your relationship with your monthly donors. For example, have a high-ranking board or staff member call the donor to thank them for being a monthly donor. For this kind of calling, you can leave a message on an answering machine if the person doesn't answer.

- You can use the phone to invite donors to special events.

- You can use the phone to survey donors: Find out if they are pleased to be a member, if they're getting what they want from you, etc.

- You can ask the callers to record biographical details that are important. For example, callers can often estimate an individual's age, or the individual may volunteer information (i.e., they just turned 65 and retired). Age is a primary factor to consider when you're approaching people about legacies or other forms of planned giving.

- You can also establish gender. The "R. MacDonald" or "Chris Beeman" on your mailing list can be identified, and addressed appropriately.

- You can call members to give them important information about urgent or special new programs. For instance, if you are an environmental organization and a logging company is doing massive clear-cuts, you can call your club donors and ask if they would help you lobby the government. This pays off in extra gifts, and stronger connections.

- You can recruit volunteers. If your callers are astute, they can identify people who might be willing to volunteer.

- You can upgrade your monthly donors by phone, and this is incredibly cost-effective.

- You can test different premiums over the phone and get instant feedback on what your donors are interested in. This could save you a lot of money in direct mail testing.

- You can update incorrect names and addresses. Too many addresses, names, and salutations are wrong. A call can help you update your records and eliminate names of people who have moved, died, or will never support your organization again for some reason. This can produce significant savings for your phone and mail programs. Your script should include an address check for everyone, whether they are Yes or No, unless they are hostile to the call.

Measuring the cost-effectiveness of telemarketing vs. direct mail

Given that a telephone call tends to be the next best thing to a person-to-person visit, you will likely recruit more members that way. However, your costs are dramatically higher than for direct mail.

It's important to compare the cost of the two, as well as how many people you recruit. You may discover that special appeals and constant reminders about your monthly giving program, in all your mailings and newsletters, will recruit enough donors to end up being as cost-effective, or more cost-effective, than telemarketing.

The other key point to compare is the fulfillment rate and how long donors last. You may find that telephone donors who pledge monthly gifts and fulfill by statement notices have a lower fulfillment rate than individuals recruited by direct mail. (Perhaps the latter are more mail-responsive than those who enter your program in response to a phone call.)

What the pros say

Joe White, vice-president of the U.S. telemarketing company Share Group, Inc., says he gets 6 to 10 percent of contacts to convert to monthly giving. He usually asks for one-year commitments, as opposed to open-ended giving.

Like all good telemarketers, his callers negotiate the monthly Ask based on a donor's giving history. In his experience, premiums have not made a huge difference. But they work well for some organizations and are used extensively by some of the most successful programs, especially religious organizations.

Joe White's callers generally don't mention EFT over the phone, whereas telemarketing consultant Rich Fox's European experience is completely different: In Europe, donors ask for EFT. Bob Penner at Canada's Strategic Communications also emphasizes EFT pledges.

Fox has found that an "earlybird" premium motivates donors to return their signed forms and therefore increases pledge fulfillment rate. You can offer this premium over the phone, or introduce it in the mail confirmation package. Fox also has found that two-person households tend to upgrade more often, perhaps because they're a stronger economic unit.

Upgrading a donor by phone

Your monthly donors have made strong commitments to your cause, and therefore they are generally far more receptive to a call asking them to increase their monthly gift—up to 40 percent. Some low-dollar monthly donors (in the $5 to $10 range) will often double their monthly gifts.

Because you already have the voided check and authorization of an EFT or credit card donor, there's no fulfillment problem in the upgrading. Still, you should send them a confirmation letter, giving them the opportunity to change their minds. Few will.

Inertia is one of the reasons people stay in a program, so when you call, it does open up the opportunity for them to cancel or downgrade their gift. Their priorities may have changed, your nonprofit may have shifted its focus, money may be tighter—there are many reasons, and cancellations will occur. Your callers need to be prepared to talk a caller out of canceling, even if it means negotiating a reduction in gift amount. If too many people cancel, look at their source of origin and the segment they come from. This will help you decide if you should stop calling a certain group. Overall, telemarketing will make more money for your organization, but you need to track it on a daily basis.

CHAPTER 10

Using newsletters, brochures, space ads, and special events to build your monthly giving program

Direct mail and telemarketing are the two most commonly used ways to build monthly giving programs. In this chapter, I want to take a look at several other very cost-effective methods. None will build a large monthly giving program by itself, but, with one exception (space advertising), they're cheap and can play a significant role over the long haul. Then, in the next chapter, we'll examine the use of person-to-person contacts, video, and broadcast media.

Newsletters

Your regular donor newsletter is an effective way to promote your monthly program. You can encourage this by printing a response coupon in the newsletter itself, by including a detached reply form when you send the newsletter, or by inserting a wallet-flap envelope that features a monthly giving option. Your donors will become more familiar with and accepting of the concept. They will be more likely to join when they receive a special invitation package or a call.

Consider creating a *special newsletter for your monthly donors*. The content of a newsletter for monthly donors shouldn't simply echo your general newsletter. You want to make the monthly donors feel special and keep them loyal to your organization. They should feel that they know where and how their money's being spent.

One of the reasons to set up a special newsletter for monthly donors is that you can address them as members of a special club. Otherwise, the newsletter you send them, while it may be very good, doesn't recognize their special status in your organization.

The frequency of a newsletter for monthly donors is partly dependent on how people give. You do not need to mail a newsletter to credit card or EFT donors more than six times a year. You may be able to mail as few as two times a year with no negative impact.

On the other hand, for billing statement donors, you may want to test sending a newsletter with the monthly bill to see how it affects response. I've seen newsletters reduce response—so be careful and test it. You may need to mail the newsletter separately to realize more net income. If you do this, be prepared for, and sensitive to, complaints of

---

I am proud to support the ongoing work of the Quilt

- ❏ FRIEND'S CIRCLE *($35 gift or pledge $5/month)*
- ❏ PANEL SPONSOR'S CIRCLE *($100 gift or pledge $10/month)*
- ❏ TWELVE BY TWELVE SPONSOR'S CIRCLE *($250 gift or pledge $25/month)*
- ❏ QUILTER'S CIRCLE *($500 gift or pledge $50/month)*
- ❏ CONSERVATOR'S CIRCLE *($1000 gift or pledge $100/month)*
- ❏ OTHER _____

❏ **Enclosed is my gift of $ _____.**   *Please make payable to The NAMES Project.*

❏ **I would like to make my gift as a monthly pledge of $ _____.**

You may have your monthly gift charged to your credit card or we would be happy to send you monthly reminders.

NAME _____

ADDRESS _____

CITY _____ STATE _____ ZIP _____

PHONE   DAY: (   )_____ EVE: (   )_____

This gift is in memory/honor of _____

Please Bill My:	CARD NUMBER	EXP. DATE
❏ Visa ❏ Mastercard	SIGNATURE	

T H A N K   Y O U

Your MEMBERSHIP CIRCLE will be based on all gifts during the current calendar year, including any gifts you have made to date. Donations to the NAMES Project Foundation are tax-deductible to the fullest extent of the law.

too much mail.

One question to ask is whether you even need a special newsletter. That depends on what kind of donors you have. If your program is all EFT, or credit card-based, the need isn't as great as it is if your donors are check-based. However, most donors do want some correspondence. They want to find out how their donations are being spent and they

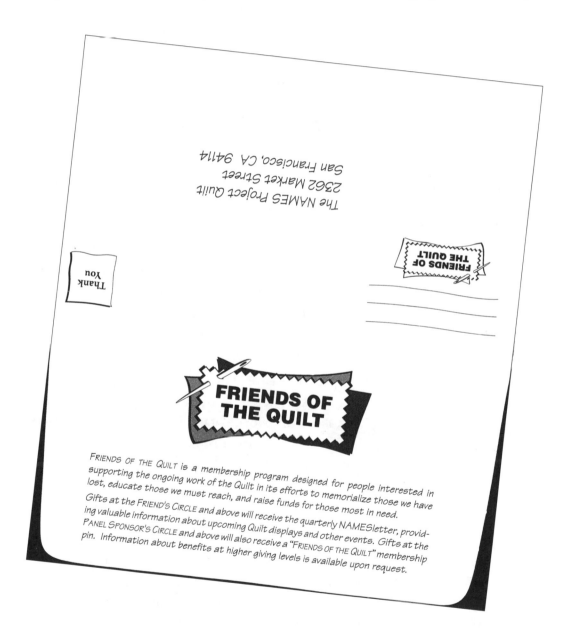

Wallet-flap reply envelope that may be distributed through newsletters, at events, or otherwise *(this page and previous)*
Illustration 10.1

like to be thanked in print for their special commitment.

The second question is at what point should you start a special newsletter? If you're slowly building a program, should you wait a couple of years before starting a newsletter? Or should you start one right away, even if there are only a few dozen donors at first?

I recommend that you first look at how fast your program is likely to grow based on early response rates. Determine how much you plan to invest in growth. And then make a decision about when it would be cost-effective to start a special newsletter for monthly donors.

In addition to actual printing and production costs, you must factor in the staff time or contracted time to write, design, and produce the newsletter. This can be a significant expense. However, evaluate it against the income that these donors will provide. If the donors are on an EFT or credit card program, they will be giving for many, many years, and a newsletter can reduce your attrition rate. But remember, most attrition, at least from EFT and credit cards, will be from change of financial circumstances, illness, and infirmity. A newsletter won't keep these individuals from dropping out.

Even if your special newsletter has no positive impact on donor retention, it is invaluable as a tool to promote planned giving. Newsletter production costs for an entire year could easily be covered by one legacy. If you have thousands of people in your monthly giving program, you have the perfect target audience for promoting legacies.

If your monthly giving program is primarily check-based, you should test sending these donors a newsletter. Design two or three different formats focusing on distinct areas of your work. Many Christian organizations do this successfully. Their donors can distinguish between packages because they are different from month to month.

"Take-one" brochures

"Take-one" brochures sit in a box on the counter in stores, in your offices, on a shelf at community centers or libraries, or in other places where people are likely to pick them up. You can use them at public events, and you can include them in letters to donors who ask for more information or when you send out tax receipts. Brochures can be a good, cheap way to find members. Over the years I've recruited hundreds of members with them.

There are two main kinds of brochures:

We
are a group of British Columbians dedicated to making sure every child and adult with a mental handicap has a chance to achieve their full potential.

Will you help give them that chance by joining our Circle of Friends?

What is the Circle of Friends?

The Circle of Friends is a special group of people who have joined the B.C. Association for Community Living (BCACL) to help people with mental handicaps. For just pennies a day you can also be a member ... and the help you give will make a real difference.

Opening doors for people with mental handicaps

Today people with mental handicaps face huge obstacles. Isolation. Poverty. Segregation. Every day families in B.C. struggle to find resources to help keep their handicapped children at home.

A small monthly donation adds up to a big change for people who rely on BCACL for help.

BCACL's goal is to make communities better places for people with mental handicaps. Your support will make this happen.

How can I join the Circle of Friends?

First you decide what you can afford to give each month. Then fill out the attached form. Your gift is automatically transferred from your chequing account to BCACL's account. Then it immediately goes to work for people with mental handicaps.

What should I give?

You decide what fits into your budget. And of course your tax-creditable gift can be changed or cancelled at any time — we guarantee it.

$10 a month is only 33 cents a day.

$20 a month is just 65 cents a day.

$30 a month is just a dollar a day.

Join the Circle of Friends and ...

... your monthly contribution will help improve the lives of many people.

It's easy for you to start.

Just fill in the attached form, and return it with one of your personal cheques, marked "VOID".

Or you can give by VISA.

That's all there is to it. Then on the first day of the month your gift is automatically transferred. Your decision can make it all happen. Please return this form to us today.

We need to expand our circle of supporters. Will you join and be a friend today!

Yes!
I will join the Circle of Friends. I authorize BCACL to draw on my chequing account or VISA credit card a monthly donation of:

☐ $10   ☐ $20   ☐ $30
☐ $50   ☐ $100   ☐ other $_____
☐ by cheque   ☐ by VISA

CARD # ☐☐☐☐☐☐☐☐☐☐☐☐☐☐☐☐

Expiry Date _____

Signature _____

NAME _____

ADDRESS _____

_____ POSTAL CODE _____

YOUR GUARANTEE: You can change or cancel your donation at any time.

PLEASE RETURN TO:

B.C. Association for Community Living
30 East 6th Avenue,
Vancouver, B.C.
V5T 4P4

With your gift you will be:

Opening minds
... by challenging deep-seated attitudes toward people who have different abilities

Opening schools
... and giving everyone access to regular classrooms

Opening homes
... to people who have spent their lives in institutions

Opening families
... creating links between people who are alone with family members and need support.

Opening horizons
... with training and support to help people with mental handicaps speak for themselves

Opening opportunity
... by promoting meaningful work for everyone.

Together we are making a difference.

Together we are building tomorrow's community.

We invite you to join our *Circle of Friends.*

BCACL

In September 1989, British Columbians for Mentally Handicapped People (BCMHP) officially changed its name to *B.C. Association for Community Living*. This change reflects our goal of making communities better places for people with mental handicaps.

Our name has changed but our programs, our vision, and our commitment to serving the needs of people with mental handicaps remains stronger than ever.

As a provincial body, *BCACL* represents local associations in almost 90 communities throughout B.C.

BCACL
30 East 6th Ave.,
Vancouver, B.C.
V5T 4P4.
Phone 875-1119.

Every person deserves a chance. Will you help give them that chance?

A project of the
British Columbia
Association for
Community Living

A brochure used to promote a monthly giving club
Illustration 10.2

- An "all-in-one" or a "self-mailer." A brochure of this type generally includes or encloses a Business Reply Envelope.
- A standard brochure, perhaps with a perforated reply form in it. In this case, the donor supplies the envelope, or you can insert a BRE in each brochure.

The advantage of the all-in-one is that donors immediately have an envelope available. However, the all-in-one tends to look cheaper than the standard brochure.

If you total up all your production costs for these brochures and balance them off against even a few donors, you'll probably see that this is a worthwhile expenditure. For instance, if the average donation to your organization is $15 a month or $180 a year, and a donor lasts for seven years, your income from one donor will be $1,260. You can print a lot of brochures for $1,260. When you recruit dozens of donors with these brochures, you'll have made a fabulous amount of money for a small investment.

Here are the essentials to include in your monthly giving brochure:

- a synthesis of your message
- your offer, clearly stated
- the exclusiveness of the club
- the premiums offered to donors
- the gift amount you're looking for
- where the donor's money will be spent
- how easy it is to join via EFT, or credit card
- how important their commitment will be to your cause

Your brochure should highlight all the benefits of participation in your monthly giving program. The reply form should be cast in a simple, straightforward style: "Yes, I want to be a member of this exclusive club." You may want to test different gift amount options. This is fairly easy to do by substituting one panel, or one side of a sheet.

If you have a fixed entry level of $10, then you want to explain how $10 makes a difference. If it's $20 a month that feeds an animal in a shelter, then you want to emphasize that. When you talk about price, it's also very important to break it down into the cost per day. A dollar a day doesn't sound like much, but that's $365 a year. Similarly, it's much easier to decide to commit 33 cents a day than $10 a month, even though it works out to the same thing.

A brochure gives you a great opportunity to use photos of your work. The cover photo and copy should make the donor want to open the brochure and continue reading. The copy should be stimulating, provocative, inviting, or it should raise a question that the prospect wants answered.

Make your reply form stand out from the rest of the brochure with a heading like "Membership Application" or "Charter Member Registration Form" at the top. This draws the reader's attention and gives the reply form some value. The copy on the reply form should restate the offer and the benefits to the donor.

Space advertising

A space ad is a mail-order advertisement that runs in a publication. You can run these in your newsletters and magazines for free. You can also buy space in newspapers and magazines. Generally, magazines are a better buy than newspapers for many reasons, but primarily because you have a more defined audience.

To use space ads effectively, you need a direct and compelling connection between a donor's monthly gift and your organization. This is why the most effective space ads are run by child sponsorship organizations. It's hard to beat getting your own "foster child" for less than a dollar a day!

Other examples of this kind of tangible connection are propositions such as, "Each $25 monthly gift will protect an acre of rain forest" or "$100 a month will pay a needy student's tuition." These are specific, targeted, and emotionally compelling.

The ads that work will continue to run. The organizations that are successful will continue to try new ads. And the publications that are successful media buys will continue to feature these ads. Track them. Study them. They're doing it right.

Marketing legend Ed Nash recommends that after you create a print ad, take your nonprofit's name out of the copy. Now decide if you could use the same copy for another charity. If your ad is not unique to your organization, if it could just as easily be used by another nonprofit, then your creative strategy will not work in the competitive marketplace.

Angels Club Membership Acceptance Form

☐ Yes, I'll join the *Angels Club* and help Hospice of Seattle provide care for terminally ill adults and children, and their families. I authorize Hospice of Seattle to transfer from my bank account the amount indicated below (minimum $5):

☐ $10.00 ($.33 a day)

☐ $15.00 ($.50 a day)

☐ $25.00 ($.83 a day)

☐ $30.00 ($1 a day)

☐ _____
      other

_____
Signature Authorizing Monthly Transfers   Date

Name _____

Address _____

_____

City/ST/Zip _____

Phone Number _____

Don't forget to include a completed check for your first month's payment.

Thank you for becoming an Angel!

YOUR GUARANTEE: You can change or cancel your monthly donation at anytime simply by calling or writing to Hospice of Seattle.

Please become an Angel to the terminally ill. Return your attached membership acceptance form today!

For Your Records:

Amount Per Month Pledged $_____

For more information please contact:

Kim Duncan
***Angels Club* Coordinator**
206-320-4000

Hospice of Seattle
425 Pontius Ave. N. #300
Seattle, WA 98109

Hospice of Seattle

Angels Club

We invite you to become a charter member

What Is The *Angels Club*?

Hospice of Seattle's *Angels Club* is a special group of individuals who commit to making a gift each month to help terminally ill adults and children, and their families. Each *Angels Club* member chooses the amount of their monthly gift.

You know that dependable monthly income makes planning easier for you. The same is true for Hospice of Seattle. The *Angels Club* is the backbone of support for our work with terminally ill patients. We hope that you will become an Angel to the people we serve.

❖ ❖ ❖

"I could not have made it through this difficult time without your care, concern, and support. You are angels for the dying."
    Hospice of Seattle Family Member

❖ ❖ ❖

Your Membership Means So Much:

1. You help us to reduce administrative costs.
2. You help us to help more people.
3. You help us to plan more effectively and to be more efficient.

4. Your *Angels Club* monthly donation provides steady, dependable support.
5. Your help enables us to care for all patients, regardless of their ability to pay.

A Little Every Month Goes A Long Way For Hospice Patients

Your monthly tax deductible gift of $15 over one year will provide a two weeks' emergency supply of medications for a patient whose funding has run out. Your monthly gift of $25 over one year will pay for a six week bereavement support group. Even a small monthly gift will provide much needed help to many people facing terminal illness and bereavement.

How The *Angels Club* Works

Your gift is automatically transferred each month from your checking account to Hospice of Seattle. *Angels Club* makes giving easy by freeing you from writing out the check, finding postage and addressing the envelope. It also means your gifts go to work immediately.
As our special thanks, we'll send you a summary statement at the end of the year showing your total giving.

❖ ❖ ❖

"You gave us not only the tools with which to care for our parents, but more importantly, the courage to do so. You must be angels!"
    Patient's Daughter

❖ ❖ ❖

Earning Your Wings:

1. Decide how much you wish to give each month.

2. Fill out the reverse side of this brochure and return it with a completed check for your first month's gift.

3. Send your form to Hospice of Seattle.

4. On or about the 20th of each month, your gift will be automatically transferred to Hospice of Seattle. Your transfers will continue until you notify us otherwise.

It's that easy. And every day, you help terminally ill adults and children live out their final days with dignity, comfort and support.

Invitation brochure for
a small nonprofit
Illustration 10.3

Space ads are often most productive as "lead generators," i.e., offering free information or a premium and thus creating an opportunity for you to respond with an invitation to join your monthly giving program. If your cause is such that you can't really tie a specific amount to a specific expenditure, then you may be better off using your ads as lead generators to acquire new names. You can ask for single gifts and even encourage people to inquire about your monthly giving program, but your goal is simply to get as many new names as possible. You then attempt to convert them later.

It's important to evaluate both of these options. The economics are quite different. Generating leads and single gifts may turn out to be less cost-effective in the long term than recruiting monthly donors, even with small numbers. It depends on your ability to convert single-gift donors to a monthly commitment.

Before you decide to run space ads to recruit monthly donors, analyze how many responses you need to break even. Accurate projections are easier if you have an established program, know what your average entry-level gift is, and have a sense of how long a donor will give.

Let's take one example. Say you spent $5,000 on an ad in a magazine with a circulation of 100,000. How many monthly donors do you need to recruit for the ad to pay for itself? If your average monthly donor is worth $1,800 over her lifetime, you only need three people to respond to your ad to make it worthwhile. In addition to getting the donors, the ad is also promoting your cause, making people more familiar with your mission. This could easily have a spill-over effect in your other fundraising or publicity efforts.

If you get more than three responses, you start making serious money.

Other things to look at are the timing and frequency: How often can you run an ad in a particular publication? Should you test different ads with different messages? Even if a certain magazine has an audience that is sympathetic to your cause, they may get bored with the ad if it runs issue after issue.

Timing is another crucial factor in your print schedule. In commercial direct response, January tends to be the best month for magazine ads; February and March are also reasonably good. September,

October, and November are generally the second best time. The second quarter tends to be bad, and the summer months are mediocre.

How do you select publications? This is always the key question. Selecting a publication is difficult without a comprehensive understanding of the magazines, a familiarity with their content, and an understanding of who their audience is. The cards that a list broker will provide won't tell you much other than perhaps age, sex, and if a list is direct mail sold. For instance, just because you're a food bank, you won't necessarily do well with people who read *Gourmet* magazine, even though they also have an interest in food! Just because a magazine is about health and the outdoors doesn't necessarily mean that its readers will respond to environmental causes.

However, you should still look for a match between your cause and the magazine's subscriber list. And check the demographics and psychographics of your donors against a subscriber list if possible. The key, of course, will be finding magazine readers who are responsive to direct marketing.

The obvious advantage of advertising is that you can reach far more people at a lower cost than direct mail. However, you will get a much lower response. Nonetheless, it can be cost-effective, especially if you can recruit people who pledge $20 or more a month.

Free-standing newspaper inserts (FSIs)

Newspaper inserts for nonprofits are relatively rare in North America, but they are quite common—and very successful—in England, where they're often found in weekend or Sunday papers. These promotional pieces could be anything from an elaborate 11" x 14" all-in-one with a bound-in reply envelope to an eight-page supplement that carries advertising. The pre-printed material is given to the publisher to insert in her publication. The insertion may be used in the entire press run or in only certain segments of it. You can have your insert go to subscribers only, to homeowners only, to specific geographical areas, and so on.

I have seen a couple of inserts done in Canada, and they probably worked because the organizations have used them repeatedly. Although newspaper inserts are quite costly, they have significant potential given the high Long-Term Value of donors who sign up for

Magazine ads may work for some causes
Illustration 10.4

your monthly giving program.

Special events, disasters, and other opportunities

For an Oxfam-Canada special event in 1982, I invited Dr. Charlie Clements to speak at a public meeting in Vancouver. Clements had just written a popular book called *Witness to War: An American Doctor in El Salvador*. A film with the same title, based on his experiences in the Salvadoran war zones, won an Academy Award for Best Documentary that year. He was an appropriate speaker, because Oxfam had humanitarian medical projects in the war zones.

We raised more than $4,000 in single gifts from 200 people present at the event. But we accomplished something even more important.

When we passed around the collection buckets, we asked people to consider becoming a monthly supporter of Oxfam's work and reminded them that an "application form" was in their event program. To increase the sign-up rate, we offered an inscribed hardcover copy of Dr. Clements' book to each new member. We got five new members at an average of $21 per month, providing $1,260 in the first year. Since these donors all signed up to give by EFT, we could anticipate that their lifetime giving would be at least $8,820—*more than double the initial money collected from the other 200 donors.*

The point of this anecdote is simple: You should always regard a special event as an opportunity to ask people to join a monthly giving program.

You can promote monthly pledges in the event's program booklet. You can insert a reply envelope with a bang-tail (or "wallet") flap that gives the individual an opportunity to sign a monthly pledge. You can offer premiums for people who join right away. And the speaker can emphasize, from the stage, how crucial and how special monthly supporters are. (Distribute forms so people can join immediately.)

Emergencies can also be great motivators. During the Ethiopian crisis of 1984, Oxfam America asked its donors to make a five-month pledge to help during this emergency period. This appeal raised more money from individuals because it allowed the donors to spread their contribution over five payments. It also served to identify individuals who were predisposed to monthly giving. Many of these donors continued their monthly giving at the end of five months. It was easy to make the argument that long-term problems need long-term solutions—and a long-term commitment. When you try to solve a problem that won't go away overnight (and what will?), this argument always applies.

During the same crisis, I designed a buckslip-sized monthly donor reply form and sent it out with thank-you letters and tax receipts to people who made a donation. We had dozens of volunteers and we organized them into many different teams. One team would phone all donors over a certain amount to thank them. Another team handwrote the donor's name and address in blue ink on the reply form. All the donors had to do was check off the amount they wanted to pledge and return the BRE. The copy read something along the lines of, "Yes, I realize that disaster prevention takes a long-term commitment. I'm willing to join Oxfam's monthly giving program to help prevent more disasters like Ethiopia." For the cost of 2,000 sheets of paper cut into 6,000 buckslips, we pulled 300 new monthly donors at a $14 average, in just two months!

Look for current events and crises that you can use for emergency appeals and recruiting opportunities. These events can help you bring attention to the overall objectives of your organization and motivate new donors to support your work. It doesn't have to be the latest California earthquake or African famine. It could be a shocking national report on child poverty, or growing violence against women. Timing is crucial, and the key is to seize an opportunity as soon as it presents itself. Monitor the media so you have a sense of which emergencies and disasters have the potential to attract coverage.

Wallet-flap reply envelopes

Wallet-flap reply envelopes have an attached, perforated flap. You can detach this from the envelope and fill out the order form that's usually printed on it. One of my clients has recruited hundreds of new monthly donors through this method alone by including wallet-flap envelopes in newsletter mailings and general correspondence.

Posters

Posters, with a packet of gummed response forms that people can tear off to make a pledge, also work for some groups. Foster Parents Plan of Canada has recruited thousands of donors this way. They put their posters in subways, on buses, and even in stores.

During the Ethiopian crisis in 1984, Oxfam-Canada quickly designed posters with stapled response forms and distributed them throughout Vancouver. We recruited 2,000 donors this way, converting approximately 5 percent directly into our monthly giving plan. Especially in emergencies, this is a very cheap and easy way to get publicity and recruit new donors. Test it in your area when appropriate.

Retail outlets

If you have a store that sells products from your organization, slip "take-one" brochures into the bags when people make purchases. This kind of distribution is free; the only cost is the brochure itself.

You might also consider approaching the owners of retail stores that might make a good match with your organization.

If you're an international development agency, for example, talk to stores that carry Third World handicrafts and suggest that they insert your brochures into their customers' bags, especially around Christmas.

If you're a food bank, you could approach your local food co-op or grocery store to see if they're willing to insert a monthly donor recruitment brochure in the bags that they distribute.

If you're a ballet company, find a store that sells dance apparel. Most nonprofits can find a match between a business operation and their organization.

Ask the business to do this for a limited time. Don't expect them to do it all year round. If they agree to participate for a two-week test period, then you'll have a better sense of how—and if—it works for your cause.

The worst-case scenario is that you spend ten cents per piece to produce a brochure that just gives you positive general advertising. And—if you pick the right stores—you will reach people who are likely to be sympathetic to your cause. In the long run, even this could result in more donations from direct mail, phone calls, or ticket sales.

CHAPTER 11

Other ways to recruit monthly donors: person-to-person contact, video, broadcast media, and online

Not long ago, Rosemary Oliver, a friend and a great fundraiser, asked me to join Greenpeace's monthly donor program. I declined, despite being a Greenpeace donor, despite our friendship, despite being on the Greenpeace Canada Board of Directors.

I declined because, in addition to giving frequent gifts to a number of causes, I'm already enrolled in three monthly giving programs.

I resisted so stiffly because a significant amount of money was already being sucked out of my checking account on the first of every month.

But being a good fundraiser, she asked me again two months after the first solicitation. I wavered, but declined. (I wasn't sure this book would sell.)

Then someone at a board meeting (a "special event") talked passionately about the world we are leaving for our children and their children. It put me in the right emotional frame of mind. I know that each of us has to take responsibility and do what we can to fight environmental degradation. And I know Greenpeace is one of the best ways to invest my money. So . . .

I passed Rosemary a note saying, "Sign me up." I added a P.S.: "This is worth much more than $10,000." Which it will be, assuming I live as long as I should, given my healthy habits and good genes.

But while moved emotionally by the speaker, I wouldn't have joined without the previous personal approach.

I know how to say No. I already had three monthly commitments, yet persistence and timing made me join a fourth program. And it would not have happened without the personal Ask. Thanks, Rosemary. And congratulations.

Person-to-person solicitation

There are three ways to organize a person-to-person monthly donor recruitment campaign:

- *Canvassing*: you can go door-to-door to recruit individuals. If you do canvass, you can either ask people to become monthly donors at the door, or try to get a single gift and establish an ongoing relationship. Later, you can contact the prospect through some other means, probably phone.

- Set up *public booths* in places where people congregate: outside a theater, at a farmer's market, etc. You can organize these with volunteers or paid individuals, or contract them out.

- Organize a *campaign-style* person-to-person campaign, with your volunteers each asking approximately four people to become monthly donors. In this type of campaign, you carefully select the prospects your volunteers will approach, decide exactly what they will ask for, and set specific goals.

All three methods may be great low-cost ways to build your monthly giving program. As a professional fundraiser, you know that the most successful way to obtain a gift is through person-to-person solicitation. And if it is feasible for you to organize a one-on-one recruiting campaign, you will have rapid growth. Many prospects and donors may never have met a representative from your nonprofit. Personal fundraising gives a human face to

This organization sends a small premium with every monthly
statement to increase the rate of fulfillment *(this page and next)*
Illustration 11.1

Cold Weather Pet Tips

 1. Keep a supply of canned/dry pet food with other emergency provisions, as well as plenty of water. In case of inclement weather, power outages, or natural disasters, your pet will always have enough food to eat.

2. Never let your dog off the leash on snow or ice, especially during a snowstorm. Dogs frequently lose their scent in the snow and ice and easily become lost.

 3. Increase your pet's supply of food, particularly protein, to keep its fur thick and healthy during the winter months.

 4. Wipe off your dog's paws when it comes out of the snow or ice to remove salt and other chemicals which can hurt its foot pads.

 5. Antifreeze, even in very tiny doses, is a lethal poison. But because of its sweet taste, animals are attracted to it. Be sure to clean up spills thoroughly.

ASPCA Guardians

Dear Guardian,

Because winter is so difficult for homeless animals, we were especially grateful to be able to count on your regular gifts these past months. Your generosity, combined with that of other Guardians, helped the ASPCA find homes for 655 unwanted animals during the month of November alone!

On behalf of the animals, thank you for your steadfast support.

With deepest gratitude,

Julie Israel

Julie Israel
Guardian Coordinator

your organization. Given the Long-Term Value of a monthly donor, recruiting on a person-to-person basis can be highly cost-effective.

Say you can recruit 40 volunteers. If each volunteer signs up three people, you will have 120 new monthly donors. With an average of just $15 a month, you'll have a yearly income of $21,600 from just these 120 monthly donors (assuming 100 percent fulfillment). If the average life span as a member is six years—and it could be much longer—the gross income will be $129,600 from this small campaign. (This calculation does not even consider upgrading or special single-gift income—and you'll raise income from both.)

How else can a nonprofit—outside of a major capital campaign— raise $129,000 from the volunteer time of 40 people each working two to eight hours? If they can put in 200 hours of volunteer time, your nonprofit earns $648 per hour—and over 90 percent of this will be net income!

Compare the total volunteer hours spent on your last special event. Compare the net income per volunteer hour. Now think about how you can re-deploy those volunteers to make much more money.

Just like any other personal solicitation campaign, your campaign volunteers must join the monthly club, otherwise they will not be able to convince someone else to join. This is essential and you must emphasize it in training.

At the very least, organizing a small campaign is the perfect way to get all the volunteers to join your monthly program!

What's the worst-case scenario? They don't recruit any monthly donors. But since volunteers have become monthly donors to be part of the campaign, look what happens. Just 40 members giving an average of $15 a month is $7,200 a year, or more than $50,000 over a seven-year period! And your volunteers are likely to give longer than the average donors.

Not bad for a disastrous campaign!

Launching a person-to-person campaign

A training session for volunteer canvassers will inspire them and provide them with the necessary skills and information to do the job. Make sure you include role-playing exercises. You need to motivate volunteers to accomplish a specific goal, and you need to provide them with "technical skills training"—how to ask and how to overcome objections.

When volunteer recruiters understand the real value of each new donor, they can become inspired. All they are asking for is $10 or $20—it just happens to be coming in each and every month to support your work. And every $10 donor could easily be worth $1,000 over a lifetime of giving.

You can select prospect names from your database, or brainstorm with volunteers to decide whom they should approach. You must cross-reference the proposed names with your database, because you do not want them accidentally downgrading a donor's giving level.

One-to-one approaches are a perfect way to promote EFT giving. The process of electronic funds transfer is easy to explain to prospects and a donor may feel more comfortable giving their banking information to your representative, whom they may already know.

It's also easy for volunteer and staff solicitors to administer EFT sign-ups. All they need is the donor's signature, monthly gift amount, and sample check. If a prospect is willing to make a monthly pledge, but prefers not to give by EFT, the solicitor should then offer credit card giving, and, as a final option, a monthly billing plan. But make sure your solicitors know how important EFT is, and why they should emphasize this option. It will help if they personally give through EFT.

Who's your audience?

Before you launch a person-to-person campaign, you have to determine who your audience is. This will vary depending on the recruitment method. If you're canvassing, you must select the geographic areas to be covered. It's unlikely you'd want to canvass in a rural community where people live half a mile apart, so we'll assume you're canvassing in a large town or city.

Testing neighborhoods and analyzing your current donor base are the simplest ways to determine who comprises your audience. If you find, for example, that a preponderance of your donor base lives on the west side of your city, then this is the area where you will be most likely to recruit monthly donors.

Similarly, if you're organizing a public booth, doing research to find out who your donors are will allow you to predict where they and like-minded people might hang out. For instance, if you work for a modern dance company and you know your donors support other arts organizations, then you would set up near a theater and gallery center, rather than choosing a booth at Billy-Joe's Annual Monster Truck and Tractor Pull.

For a person-to-person campaign, knowing your audience means selecting good prospects from your donor base, or having an evaluation committee determine who your solicitors should ask and what they should ask for. Volunteers should be part of this process, because they may already know four individuals who currently don't support your organization but whom they feel might be willing to become monthly donors.

Who makes the Ask?

You have the choice of using volunteers or paid individuals for any of these campaigns, and this is something you may want to test for your organization. There are many organizations, especially in Europe, that hire individuals to do public recruitment of monthly donors. It is common for organizations to pay their canvassers, especially organizations that have year-round canvasses. For most organizations in most communities, it's not feasible to have volunteers going year-round.

Recruiting volunteers "methods and success" will vary from organization to organization. If you already have a successful volunteer program, then you should recruit from those individuals first. Don't forget to involve your board members: They may also be able to recruit other individuals. A board member or senior person on your fundraising committee should lead the campaign, if possible.

You can organize a person-to-person program in many ways, but modeling it on a capital campaign is a good choice. A board or fundraising committee member should lead your volunteer team. You develop a pyramid structure of responsibility. You set a specific target and give each member of the team two to six people to recruit. Volunteers then realize that their responsibilities are few. They know that with just a few hours of work they can fulfill their responsibility and make a positive contribution to your cause.

All your volunteers must have already enrolled in your monthly giving club! Only that way can they say, "That's why I've personally joined the program."

Creating the materials you need for your solicitors

To begin with, you need to develop a recruiting kit for volunteers. It should include:

- general information on your organization
- specific information on your monthly giving program
- EFT and credit card details if you offer them

- sign-up forms
- a list of what different monthly gifts can accomplish ("$10 a month will buy…")
- stories of how donors help, where the money is spent
- guidelines on how to ask for a commitment

You should also provide the canvasser with annual reports, so they can answer basic questions and give the prospect a report when appropriate.

One successful example of person-to-person monthly donor fundraising

One small organization with dramatic success in recruiting monthly donors on a person-to-person basis is the New Democratic Party of British Columbia. The province of British Columbia has a population of 3.8 million people spread out over an area the size of California. Half of that population lives in and around Vancouver. The NDP has been able to recruit volunteer fundraisers who go door-to-door to prospects selected from mailing lists, friends, and people who seem to be leaning towards the NDP in their voting behavior. These highly motivated volunteers have recruited thousands of donors over the years.

Raising money can be fairly easy when a party is out of power, but when they're in power and doing things that may be unpopular, it can have a devastating effect on fundraising. Direct mail or telemarketing programs may suffer greatly if the party makes unpopular decisions. However, the drop-off rate among credit card or EFT donors will still tend to be very low.

Using video to build your monthly giving program

You can gain access to the powerful medium of television in two ways:

- By buying time on television for direct response ads or infomercials, or acquiring a station-sponsored telethon.
- By producing videos and giving them to people to view at their leisure.

Producing videos is a great way of using the power of television without having to buy expensive time, or missing your audience (because they can't tune in at the time you air your show).

Video gives you the opportunity to speak directly to your donors at a time that's convenient for them. An infomercial might air when they are asleep or their kids are screaming and dinner is burning, but your video can be viewed at their leisure, when they can give it their attention.

Video is cheaper than television

Because of technological developments, video is dramatically cheaper to produce and duplicate than it was even two years ago. This allows nonprofits to mail out or distribute videos on a cost-effective basis. Relatively few nonprofits use videos to communicate with donors, but many more will do so in the future.

Video can be a powerful fundraising tool. Organizations ranging from political parties to environmental groups use direct mail videos and have seen a dramatic increase in average gift size and response rates. I have produced videos for nonprofits that have recruited monthly donors and reactivated lapsed donors. I've also been able to more than double a donor's gift and quadruple response rates using video as a fundraising tool.

In a recent election, I mailed 10,000 videos to political donors in British Columbia. The mailing dramatically increased the money raised, which in turn, helped win the election. People who had given up on the party decided, after seeing the video, to vote for them after all—and send in a contribution. If properly promoted, videos can also create many other spin-off benefits, such as valuable news stories. Video works because you get directly into people's homes with a highly personal message in a unique and incredibly powerful format. An effective video harnesses this power by matching powerful images with an engaging script and moving music to sell your nonprofit's solutions to problems.

Researchers at the Wharton Business School at the University of Pennsylvania discovered that "video brochures":

- Increase memory retention of information by 70 percent over printed materials.

- Reduce the time it takes for a viewer to make a buying decision by 72 percent, compared to print.

A well-produced video can serve your organization in two ways. It can help you build donor loyalty and recruit monthly donors. A video does everything a letter can do, but with more power. You can say much more in a video than you can in most fundraising letters or telephone calls, because you're communicating both orally and visually. This allows you to:

- explain in detail how monthly donor programs work

- display and promote any special premiums you offer

- thank donors for their support

- give prospects and donors a powerful emotional and visual sense of the work you do

There are at least eight advantages of using video:

- Video gives you the power of television.

- Donors perceive videos as having value.

- Video has the capacity to convey powerful images.

- Video projects an image of professionalism.

- Video allows you to paint a clear picture of need.

- Sending a video is a form of donor recognition.

- Video is a great tool to educate donors and prospects.

- People hold onto videos. (How many of your donors save your direct mail appeals?)

You need to send a letter with your video

Whether you hand-deliver or mail your video or send it in a FedEx package, it's crucial to include a short letter to your donor or prospect. The letter should explain why it is so important that the donor watch the video as soon as possible, and it should also make a monthly donor pitch. The basics of good direct mail apply to this letter. You can learn these by carefully reading these great books: *Dear Friend* by Kay Lautman and Henry Goldstein, and two books by Mal Warwick, *Raising Money by Mail* and *How to Write Successful Fundraising Letters*.

After you send the video you have a few options: Do nothing—just wait for the money to roll in. Or follow up by phone. This call is to ensure that people received the video and viewed it; to answer any questions that they may have; and to ask for a monthly gift. Your third option is to follow up with a reminder letter saying, "We haven't heard from you. I hope you've had an opportunity to watch the video. If you haven't received the free video, please give us a call at this toll-free number and we'll send you one." You should also restate the importance of a monthly donor program and ask for a commitment.

Videos that failed

Many businesses and nonprofits have embraced video as a selling tool, and have failed. They failed for three reasons:

- They didn't give people a reason to watch.

- They didn't ask for money properly.

- They didn't provide a way to respond—either a reply card or envelope, or a toll-free number.

On top of these reasons, many neglected to give viewers *new information*. The informational approach is a way to keep people viewing. People will continue watching if they feel they are getting potentially valuable or useful information.

What does video cost?

You can duplicate videos for less than $2 a cassette. But because a professional seven-minute video may cost $25,000 to produce, costs can still be prohibitive for your organization.

Using television advertising to build your monthly giving program

There are three basic television formats:

- short ads (30-, 60-, and 120-second spots), serving either to reinforce other fundraising efforts, to generate leads, or to solicit gifts directly (usually in 2-minute ads)

- half-hour and hour-long infomercials, which have proven most cost effective for international aid organizations and religious broadcasters

- telethons and on-air appeals (i.e., muscular dystrophy, children's hospitals, and PBS) have raised billions of dollars. But be forewarned: It's very difficult to break into this type of television.

To produce and air a television show, there are three kinds of costs:

- the initial production cost to create your 2-minute ad or 60-minute program. This cost will vary depending on the length, the quality of your production team, and how long it takes to make. "Shooting" in Africa will cost more than a local shoot. A 2-minute spot can cost $5,000 to $50,000; a half-hour from $50,000 to $250,000.

- the back-end costs of the inbound telemarketing calls: long distance charges, credit card percentages, sending out notices, updating databases, etc.

- buying media time.

Production is essentially a fixed cost, while the back-end expenses and media time costs are variable. The cost of television time is contingent on how many markets you buy and at what price. However, you will continue to buy time only if you find it profitable. To some extent, this makes calculating cost-effectiveness a difficult proposition. If your show works in test markets, it will likely succeed in roll-outs. Then you will amortize all of your fixed production costs over the lifetime of the television buys.

Remember, despite the fact that an hour-long show is 60 times as long as a one-minute spot, it does not cost 60 times as much. It may only cost you five times as much, depending on your production values and many other factors.

Television has proven to recruit monthly donors

Television evangelism, in particular, has cultivated hundreds of thousands, probably millions, of monthly donors. More importantly, it introduced the concept to vast audiences. The downside of this familiarity could be that highly religious audiences have already pledged their limit on monthly giving clubs, since televangelists have aggressively promoted this for many years.

For religious broadcasters and other nonprofits, television has also pulled in tens of millions of single-gift donors, many of whom later convert to monthly giving by mail or phone programs.

Nonprofit organizations such as World Vision, the Humane Society of Toronto, and many hospitals have been airing infomercials for many years with good results—otherwise they wouldn't continue to buy the air time!

Although these paid direct response shows will try to obtain single-gift donors, the enormous Long-Term Value of a monthly donor is obvious to these groups, and their primary pitch to viewers is simple—give monthly and you will solve a problem. And the viewers do. For instance, World Vision has more than one million donors who sponsor children for $27 a month. Television has been their prime prospecting tool.

Do you have the right cause for television?

Before you buy a video camera, ask yourself the following questions to determine your organization's potential in the direct response television field:

- Do you have adequate investment money to produce a high-quality television spot? Will you have enough money to air it, too? Can you handle all the back-end processing?

- Do you have an appeal to a large audience or significant niche markets in many areas of the country that will justify a large expenditure on a television show?

- Can you acquire monthly donors or just single gifts? If you can acquire monthly donors, your show will be far more cost-effective than with single gifts.

- Can you reach a new audience that you can't reach through your traditional media, such as direct mail and telemarketing?

- Have you got a compelling offer to make to an audience?

- Can you tie a monthly pledge to a significant part of your program that makes it appealing for viewers to pledge?

- Is your television audience capable of making monthly pledges in amounts that will allow you to cover your costs?

- How do you compare with the competition? Do you have a unique selling message that distinguishes you from other organizations in your field?

- Do you have high name recognition? For example, if you're a new child sponsorship organization competing against "brand names," you may have a very difficult time on television, unless you position yourself differently. (A few years ago, an organization was trying to enter the child sponsorship field. Their marketing stroke of genius was to offer child sponsorship at $10 a month when other organizations were offering it at $18 and $20 a month. This allowed them to reach a new market of individuals who could not afford or were unwilling to make a larger commitment. (Of course, this begs the question of what it actually costs to "sponsor" a child and where the money goes.)

- Does your organization do work that can be attractively or powerfully packaged: kids, animals, drama, success, a disaster?

- Do you have compelling stories to tell?

- Can you clearly show how a donor's gift helps?

- Can you produce a television show that works over at least several years? (Only through many successful airings can you cover your production costs and make your show profitable.)

- Do you have premiums that appeal to your prospective donors, or something they can feel emotionally connected to? For instance, child sponsorship agencies send pictures of the child you sponsor and you get regular letters from them. Environmental organizations can send a certificate showing that you've purchased an acre of rain forest for $25 to protect it forever. These small premiums enhance the value of your offer.

A toll-free number is essential to success

To make the best use of television, you need an "inbound" 800, 888, or 877 telephone operation organized well in advance. Using an in-house operation is problematic. That's why almost every organization uses a service bureau that operates 24 hours a day.

You quickly discover if it's working

One of the great advantages of television is that you can measure cost-effectiveness rapidly. When you go on the air, you know that within a number of days you'll have all your income, or all your leads. In direct mail you often have to wait weeks to find out if a mailing is successful and then it takes weeks or months to do your roll-out. In television you can often know the day after a broadcasting spot whether you made money or not, and then quickly buy other time slots.

You also know to a fair extent what worked and what didn't. If the first half of your show produces no calls and the second half, which is designed differently, produces a lot of response, you know it's time to change the first half of the show.

Radio—another broadcast medium to consider

While the focus of the last few pages has been on television, you can apply many of the principles outlined here to radio—and recruit new donors as well. Radio lacks the images, but good radio can allow people to paint their own powerful pictures in their minds.

Radio has been used by Christian evangelists with great success. And some have found that radio is more cost-effective, but they can only buy so much, so television is also an essential buy. Radio stations that target particular audiences, especially upscale audiences, may be useful for cultural organizations as a way to recruit monthly donors. And the advantage of radio is that it is incredibly cheap to do professionally, in comparison to television.

At a conference a few years ago, Jim Lavin, who works with Jerry Falwell, revealed that radio was more cost-effective than television for their ministry.

And they converted many donors to their monthly club through radio programs.

Radio is cheaper to produce and therefore there are fewer risks. If you consider radio, you have to determine how you can reach your audience through a particular station in your market and if you have a case that is compelling enough to motivate people to pick up their phone or pen. Radio can be an inexpensive way to test how appealing your offer is, but remember it is a different medium than television and you have to verbally paint pictures for people.

When you use radio, stick to the basics: Make it personal, give donors a reason to give, make a specific Ask, offer benefits if appropriate, and have an effective and efficient back-up to respond to questions and gifts.

The road more traveled

When the editor of this book asked me to write a section on monthly donor promotion on the Internet, I thought, "What can I say that won't be outdated before the yogurt in my fridge?"

I realized I should focus on fundraising and communications principles, because there are few things that are changing as fast as the Internet.

We learn new information about the World Wide Web every month: what works, what doesn't, who's succeeding, and what we should (or shouldn't) test. As Chris Paterson of Times Direct Marketing says: "There are no experts, only leaders. There is very little history, only ongoing experimentation. And there are no proven markets, only evolving prototypes."

When it comes to the Internet, it's difficult to see into my crystal ball—perhaps because of the snowflakes (I do live in Canada, as you know).

Naturally, sooner or later, every nonprofit organization will need to embrace the Internet as a marketing tool. Yet, so far, few organizations have raised significant income from the Net.

Wired households have a 50 percent higher income on average than other households in North America. We know they are readers. We know that Net "surfers" are searching for things that interest them. We know that nonprofit organizations interest the public. And we know that if we use successful direct marketing techniques online, we can acquire donors and leads.

However, unlike mail and telephone fundraising, which require very little action from a donor—only writing a check, or signing a form, or giving a credit card number, and dropping an envelope into the mailbox—

Monthly Giving Program

Programs

- Recycling Program
- Monthly Giving Program
- Planned Giving Program
- Sunshine Coach Program
- Gold Heart Day Program
- Cash for Kids Program

The Monthly Giving Program is an easy way for individuals to make an automatic monthly donation to Variety Club throughout the year. By prior arrangement a specified amount of money authorized by an individual is automatically deducted from the individual's bank account, Visa, or Mastercard on the 28th day of the month, with the proceeds going to Variety Club in support of our many programs to assist British Columbia's children with special needs.

To sign up for the Monthly Giving Program, or for more information, please call the Variety Club office at (604) 320-0505 or 1-800-381-2040.

Young Daniel Yanko and his good buddy John McKeachie, sportscaster at BCTV

Home   About Us   Programs   Where the Money Goes   Telethon   Special Events   Search   Index

©1998 Variety Club

Last updated on April 08, 1998
Web design and development by Steeves and Associates

A Web page promotion for monthly giving
Illustration 11.2

online promotion requires a prospective donor to invest a little more *time* to find your site.

Some nonprofits—ranging from the Christian Children's Fund (CCF) to Greenpeace Canada—have acquired monthly donors (as well as single-gift donors) online. Each month, CCF acquires an average of ten new $21/month child sponsors from its Web site and receives another 40 requests for information packages. (These names are then put into a "lead-cultivation" program and treated as "hot prospects.") So there's evidence that a Web site can be effective.

One of your main goals on the Web should be to build your prospect and donor database. Monthly giving, while offered as an option, should be secondary to collecting names, first-time gifts, cultivation of potential donors, and education of the public. Your Web site can reinforce your other communications via direct mail, a newsletter, and other means. But you must publicize your site on your letterhead, in TV ads, in your newsletter, and at every other opportunity that presents itself.

A Web site also creates opportunities to provide information to existing donors and strengthen their bonds with your organization. You can use a Web site to extend invitations to special events, to post surveys, to involve your donors in lobbying, and to provide access to your organization's publications.

CHAPTER 12
Getting the greatest value from your monthly donors

I hope by now I've persuaded you that your organization receives tremendous value from its monthly donors. There are six ways to maximize that value:

- Ensure that their "fulfillment rate" (the reliability with which donors send their gifts in full and on schedule) is the highest it can possibly be.
- Keep them giving loyally for as long as they possibly can.
- Secure additional gifts from them, over and above their monthly contributions.
- "Upgrade" them annually—i.e., increase their money gift amount.
- Sell them special event tickets, merchandise, or services.
- Persuade them to leave legacy gifts, by remembering your organization in their wills or arranging for other forms of planned gifts.

In a well-managed monthly giving program, you'll simultaneously pursue every one of these possibilities, if it makes sense for your organization. In this chapter, I'll touch on each of these tactics in turn.

But always keep this principle in mind: *Treat your monthly donors the way they want to be treated!*

Maximizing fulfillment rates

In designing your monthly giving program, one of the earliest and most significant questions you'll face is whether to exempt monthly donors from other fundraising efforts. Many organizations do so (at least up to a point). Some donors regard the promise of escape from otherwise frequent appeals to be a major selling point for monthly giving.

I believe the best approach is to recognize a donor's new status. You should make all such decisions on the basis of this proposition: Monthly donors are special. Once someone responds to your invitation to join a monthly giving club, it is important to highlight that "specialness" by distinguishing the club from your organization's other fundraising programs.

How to handle donors who pay by check

For donors who pay by check, the most widespread method of monthly giving in the United States, consider taking the following steps:

1. *Take monthly donors out of the regular mailing stream.*

   Once you're informed that a donor has joined your monthly giving club, enter a special code in his record that indicates: *no annual renewals or special appeals.* Continuing to mail these routine solicitations may result in an increase in short-term net income, but not much of an increase. The problem is, these appeals will confuse your donor and disrupt any system you establish to track the returns from your monthly giving program.

   Most importantly, continuing to send annual or special appeals will undermine the donor's special status as a valuable club member. (That said, you might want to offer him the option of receiving *all* the mail from your organization. A few of your monthly donors will want everything you can send them.) I know of only one organization that makes more money by sending all appeals. But I suspect this could ultimately result in a much lower donor lifetime value.

   I also recommend sending your newsletter to monthly givers, assuming you don't already send one with the monthly statement or have a special newsletter for club members that's mailed separately. It's good to mail a copy of your annual report as well.

   Remember: Monthly donors will respond best if you treat them as the special folks they are.

2. *Create a billing file, so each donor will receive a statement every month.*

   Ideally, your monthly donor billing file will not be a separate file, but will be integrated with your database. This will reduce the chances that a club member will receive prospect or house mailings.

Share *Plan*

Winter 1988 • Volume 2 Number 1

A special newsletter exclusively for SharePlan members!

A year of growth

by Meyer Brownstone
Oxfam Canada chairperson

Thank you for your generous support of Oxfam-Canada during 1987. It was a year where support for our work increased.

Welcome to 600 new members!

SharePlan membership grew by 600 people to 3,300 Canadians!

This is very encouraging to me and to the other volunteers and staff of Oxfam. It means we can fund more projects so more people are helped and through this there is a little more justice in our world.

But while this is extremely positive, I'm afraid I must report to you that we start 1988 with a deficit.

As you probably realize the postal interruption of last fall adversely affected many organizations whose donors reach them by mail.

Oxfam was no exception. As a result we begin the year with a deficit we must overcome.

We barely had time to get an emergency message in the Christmas mailing. You may have been one of many donors who responded with great generosity to that note. If so, I thank you. The result of the extra funds received at Christmas means we have a much smaller figure to make up.

The real value of your **SharePlan** donation was wonderfully clear during the postal interruption. It means Oxfam is not totally dependent on the mail for its income.

We will work hard to erase this deficit and I believe we will succeed. Let me thank you in advance if this year you decide to increase your monthly donation.

Thanks again for being the backbone of Oxfam's work and let me extend my best wishes to you during 1988. •

This powerful graphic is on a postcard designed by Oxfam (U.K.) to raise funds for projects.

OUR CULTURE OUR FREEDOM OUR RIGHTS OUR FAMILY WAY OF LIFE ARE ALL ROOTED IN OUR LAND

Survey response

Thanks to all of you who completed Oxfam's donor survey. The response was tremendous and very gratifying. We are now compiling the results and will have a full report for you in our next newsletter in the early fall.

Preliminary responses are fascinating. But we'll save the details for a full report in the next issue of Shareplan.

Chile: struggling for a future

by Paul Mably
Program Development Officer
Andean Region

Ana Maria has raised her son alone. He's now a teenager and can lend a hand. For both of them it means doing odd jobs. On the island of Chiloe in southern Chile there is no full-time work.

They live in a wooden shack in a green valley planted with potatoes and dotted with sheep. Most of the fields and sheep belong to a few large landholders.

Chile

Ana Maria's plot of land is smaller than the average suburban Canadian back yard. She cannot depend on it for her food needs, much less to produce a marketable surplus.

Others in the village of Bio-Bio had the same problem. They started to talk about it with the village priest who called on the Chiloe Development Office (OPDECH in Spanish).

Continued on page 2

Share *Plan* #3

SharePlan is a special twice-a-year newsletter for Shareplan members.

Your copy of Oxfam-Canada's annual report for the 1986-1987 fiscal year will be mailed to you in April. This allows us to get your tax receipt to you much sooner.

A newsletter mailed exclusively to monthly donors
Illustration 12.1

Despite your best efforts to avoid sending prospect packages to your monthly donors (or any other group of human beings with mailing addresses), they'll get them anyway. So, whenever a donor complains, make sure you record any variation in spelling or format of their name or address a special "kill file" or "eliminator file" (a database file that ensures donors will not be selected for inclusion in a mailing). For instance, if a club member named *Steve Currie* received a prospect letter addressed to him as *Steve Curry*, make a kill file record of that misspelled name. You may even want to be proactive and add some of the obvious variations of a member's name to your own kill file.

3.   *Print up the monthly statements with special messages tailored to each donor's particular status (e.g., up-to-date, one-month lapsed etc.).*

Mail monthly statements to check donors to arrive about one week before the end of each month. Monitor and test the exact timing, which may vary depending on whether your organization is local, regional, or national.

Ideally, monthly statements should be sent via first class mail, but if your list is very large, you may want to test the effect of using bulk mail on your response rates.

Your goal is to get an invoice into the hands of each donor so that when she pays her monthly bills, you're in the "to-be-paid" stack along with the phone, rent or mortgage, and water bills. You must mail monthly statements on time—every month. Otherwise, your response rate (fulfillment) will drop significantly.

If yours is a small organization, take special care not to "miss" a month simply because the only staff person who knows how to prepare the statements is either sick or on vacation. Similarly, you may want to mail a few days early in heavy mailing months just to ensure your statements arrive on time.

4.   *Make sure that monthly donor reply envelopes are easily distinguished from your regular reply envelopes.*

Specially printed or coded reply envelopes will make gift processing far easier and reduce errors in coding. It's ideal to designate one person to handle the data entry for all your monthly donors. As many of my clients have discovered, such a person will get to "know" the donors, often remarkably well, even though they may manage a file of 6,000 or more individuals. Familiarity of this sort will make a difference to your donors. You'll have the best results of all if you "introduce" monthly donors to the designated staff member by mail or phone, so they'll know whom to contact if a problem or a question arises.

A few words of advice to the small organization: If you manage your monthly giving program with in-house volunteer or staff labor, take advantage of the opportunity to add handwritten personal notes to your club members. Each note will only take a few seconds, but the effort will guarantee that your monthly donors feel closer to your cause. (Be sure you address donors by name, rather than adding general notes that could look computer-generated.) A personal note may be written directly on a donor's statement or attached on a Post-It note.

Communicating with EFT and credit card donors

A monthly giving program for donors who give by check almost always requires monthly mailings. In the case of EFT and credit card donors, for whom monthly mailings aren't necessary, it's all too easy to overlook a fundamental question: If you're not actively appealing to them for additional gifts by mail, phone, or other means, what *are* you doing to keep your monthly donors well-informed and continue building the intimate, long-term relationship that lies at the heart of successful fundraising?

Here, too, different approaches prevail:

- A few nonprofit organizations continue to mail every house appeal to EFT and credit card donors. They do *not* make special provisions for their electronic donors. (A top staffer at one of these organizations might write to her monthly donors, explaining that she wants to be sure they stay fully informed and receive all the information everyone else gets.)

- Other organizations send very few letters to monthly donors. They may make exceptions for an annual report or an occasional upgrade letter (perhaps not even one a year).

- Some organizations create special newsletters for their monthly donors. Alternatively—or even, occasionally, in addition to a newsletter—they might put monthly sustainers on a schedule to receive special information mailings.

As you can see, you have a great deal of latitude here. The best approach will depend on your cause and on how you want to treat your donors. My advice is to *ask the donors* how they want to be treated.

Let your monthly donors tell you what kind of information they want to receive. The ideal method is to send a short questionnaire to each new monthly donor immediately after he joins your program. Ask him what kind of mail he'd like to receive, how often, and so on. You'll probably find that some donors want to get everything. Others want nothing but a statement or tax receipt at the end of the year. By giving donors this option, you'll keep them happy, and they'll reward you by continuing to give.

When you design such a questionnaire, be very specific about what options you're offering. For example, if you mail one newsletter to your general donor file and a different one to the members of your monthly giving club, you might offer the option of receiving one newsletter, both, or neither. Offer to send them no mail—other than their annual receipt, and the thank-you that accompanies this mailing. (This may be especially important for environmental causes, many of whose donors may be deeply concerned about receiving printed material they don't want.)

Some fundraisers argue that they don't care what donors want: They know that if they keep sending more appeals, they'll raise money over and above the EFT gifts. This may be true. But focus on the long term. I believe that a sophisticated upgrade program and sending special appeals only when there's an emergency will net you more money over the lifetime of the donor.

The number of special appeals you send to your donors depends, to some extent, on the size of their gifts. For individuals at the $10 level, you might consider sending quite a number of special appeal mailings.

People on EFT programs don't actually think about their gifts every month, so if they really like your organization, they could easily make extra gifts during the year. But be very careful with this: If donors feel you're exploiting them for that extra $20, you might lose them altogether!

Here's what's at stake: Assume seven years of giving is the life-span for the average monthly donor. In that case, irritating a $10/month donor by sending too much mail or making too many phone calls might induce her to cancel her membership. As a result, you could lose a large portion of her "life-long" contributions of $840. That's a lot to lose for trying to extract an extra $20 gift! (Not to mention that you can forget that generous legacy you were counting on!)

Reminders

A guy has some friends over for dinner one evening. His friends are worried about his memory lapses, but when the subject comes up, the guy says, "I know you're worried about my memory. I've been worried, too. That's why I took this fantastic memory course—just three nights, and I learned all these techniques to memorize things. My mind's been like a steel trap ever since."

Friend says, "So what's the name of the course?" Guy pauses, looks thoughtful, scratches his head, and asks, "What's the name of that bush with the thorns and the red flowers on top?" Friend hesitates and says, "Rose?" Guy lights up and says, "Right." He turns towards the kitchen and yells, "Hey, Rose, what was the name of that course I took?"

I repeat this joke because fundraising is all about memory. You have to remember your donors' giving history—and you have to remind them to give! Most donors have no idea exactly when they last gave you a gift. You have to constantly remind them.

Has an organization ever contacted you to remind you that you haven't given in 19 months? If so, you probably could have "sworn" it was just six or seven months ago that you wrote them a check—and, of course, you have a great memory. Well, think of your donors, most of them probably older folks whose memories may not be what they once were. *Try to remember this.* It's important. And if you need help, just ask Rose to remind you. (While you're at it, don't forget to remind your monthly invoice donors *every month* about the commitment they've made.)

Depending on many factors—such as your cause, the kind of people on your list, and the effectiveness of your program—60 to 90 percent of your monthly-invoice club members will "fulfill" their gifts each month.

Dave Watson from the Southern Poverty Law Center tells me that 90 percent of their statement donors fulfill each month. Clearly, the high level of fulfillment shows that members of the Center's giving club are emotionally committed to the Center's mission and have confidence their money is being spent on programs that make a difference.

Components of a monthly reminder mailing

Generally, a monthly reminder mailing includes just four essential components: the outer envelope, the reply envelope, the billing invoice or statement, and a message to the donor. But many organizations add inserts. Let's consider each of those in turn:

The outer envelope

Do you want to send the donor the same outer envelope each month, so that they know it's their "monthly bill"? You might want to test to see if donor recognition of their "monthly bill" affects their response rate. Many organizations send the same outer envelope every month with different teaser copy that refers to the contents of an insert.

The reply envelope

Some charities believe they need a two- or three-color reply envelope to catch donors' attention. In reality, donors aren't likely to base their fulfillment decisions on the number of colors on the envelope. What's more effective is to print on the envelope the month the pledge is due.

I also recommend you test a postage-paid return envelope (BRE) against one that requires the donor to affix a stamp. The general rule is this: Low-dollar monthly donors should pay for their own postage (and probably will). Donors of larger sums may be happy to supply the stamps as well, but that proposition is worth testing.

If you routinely ask donors to affix their own stamps, you could try switching to BREs once a donor has fallen behind in her monthly payments.

The billing notice

There are eight important elements in each billing notice:

- *Donor name and address:* The name and address are commonly designed to show through a window envelope. Very few nonprofits use closed-face envelopes for their monthly donor program.

- *Billing statement title:* These invoice-like forms are labeled: Reply Card, Invoice, Reminder, etc. There are two types: One has a reply form that you return with your check. The other type has two perforated parts, the return and donor record portions.

- *Pledge amount:* This is the amount the donor has promised as a monthly gift.

- *Statement of account:* This is a statement of the donor's year-long record of fulfillment.

- *Organization's name and address*

- *Name of the monthly club* (if you have one)
- *Thank-you*
- *A donor message*

Your donor message

The messages you send monthly donors can make a significant difference in the rate of response to your program. Each month, you must motivate donors to *take action*.

A donor message usually appears at the bottom of the statement. Generally, it's limited to three to five lines. Messages may vary, falling into one or another of the following self-explanatory "Action Areas":

- Urgency
- Thank-you
- Recognition of advance pledge payment
- Acknowledgment of an extra gift
- Recognition of a donor's length of participation in the program
- Seeking to renew a donor who has missed one month
- Trying to recapture a donor who has missed a few months
- General praising of the donor
- Seasonal or holiday-specific
- Promoting EFT or credit card giving
- Promoting an insert
- Promoting a premium

The message should vary according to the donor's status, seasonal factors, and your program priorities.

When is a monthly donor "lapsed"?

Nonprofits with lower fulfillment rates should check to see if long-lapsed pledge donors are still calculated as active donors. When I started working with a large nonprofit a few years ago, they thought their monthly fulfillment rate was 60 percent. However, to calculate this figure they included people who had pledged, made one gift, and hadn't given again in 18 months! By eliminating deadwood, their actual fulfillment rate jumped to 80 percent. There was still room for improvement, but at least the 80 percent figure accurately reflected the real fulfillment level in their monthly donor file.

The decision as to when a monthly pledge donor becomes lapsed varies from charity to charity, but is generally between one and six months. The criteria I prefer are as follows:

1 month	not lapsed
2-3 months	lapsing
4-5 months	lapsed
6+ months	seriously lapsed*

* Probably gone forever unless they've been multi-year members

Many donors take long summer vacations. Some must cope with kids on summer break. Others get swamped in December and January with holidays, family, and Christmas bills. These are common times for donors to fall behind on their payments.

Most donors who are one month behind in payment are not planning to stop giving. Sometimes they mail their checks late for good personal reasons. Occasionally a check is late because of post office delays. Finally, some charities calculate that if a check hasn't been returned by Day 21 after the notice has been mailed, the donor is "behind by a month." In any case, there's little cause for concern.

When a donor is three or four months lapsed, it's time to start worrying. Special attention is required to bring them back into the fold.

When five or six months have gone by and you've heard nothing from a donor, chances are strong that he's gone forever. I'll talk about how to retrieve the two- to six-month lapses later in this chapter.

High drop-off rates may be caused by boredom or bother: Members of a monthly giving club may be turned off by constant reminders that they've made a commitment. That's one reason why it's important to vary the messages you add to their statements. Perhaps only 10 to 20 percent of your club members are bored or bothered, but unless you consider these factors, your attrition rate will increase.

Converting donors from invoice to electronic giving programs

Statement donors typically have higher rates of attrition than do EFT or credit card donors—primarily because it's simply easier to stop giving. All the donor need do is ignore a reminder mailing. By contrast, EFT or credit card donors must take action to stop giving.

As you know by now, converting check donors or even credit card donors to Electronic Funds Transfer is a great way for your organization to make more money. Of all the recommendations in this chapter to help you increase your income, an aggressive conversion campaign is the most likely to increase profits.

As I noted in Chapter 7, it's ideal to survey monthly donors who give by check. Find out why they do so, and whether (and why) they're hesitant to give through EFT or credit cards. You can then address their concerns.

If a donor objects because he likes to keep control over his account, emphasize that he *does* have complete control and can change or cancel his monthly gift at any time. Be sure to note that—depending on your EFT service provider or bank—you'll need anywhere from two days' to two weeks' notice to arrange the cancellation. (I recommend you state that you prefer two weeks' notice to ensure that all the paperwork is filled out.)

If a donor gives you insufficient time to cancel an upcoming EFT transaction, offer to repay that month's deduction. Few people will take you up on this offer. But it's important to extend it, because it's an honorable thing to do—and when you do, you'll make the donor understand that you consider his needs first. Such an offer also decreases the possibility that the donor will bad-mouth you. And it dramatically increases the chance that he'll continue giving you gifts—and perhaps someday rejoin the program.

Mail

Your direct mail program offers many opportunities to promote electronic giving. For example, you can:

- Place promotional copy for EFT on monthly statements, offering an opportunity for the donor to convert.

- Include frequent package inserts promoting EFT.

- Send a special request by letter four months after a person joins, and then once a year.

- Promote EFT in your newsletter. (Profile individuals who were hesitant to switch to EFT payments but have since found it to be an incredible convenience. Testimonials like this are a great way to address the security concerns of donors.)

- Promote EFT when you do a special letter to upgrade a donor's monthly gift.

Phone

Similarly, you can promote conversion to EFT by telephone:

- Mention conversion when you call up a donor to thank her for joining the program and to confirm an address or gift details.
- Offer conversion during phone upgrades.
- Test a special conversion call.

It's also worthwhile asking donors face-to-face to convert to EFT. At a special event, you might invite check donors to sign up for EFT, with trained volunteers ready to help them or answer their questions.

Improving your fulfillment rate through testing

If you have 10,000 monthly donors giving by check and their average pledge is $10 per month, then your monthly income will be $100,000—if they all send in their checks. Of course, they won't all do so, but you want to get as close to 100 percent as possible. Every percentage point makes a big difference. Fulfillment at 70 percent versus 80 percent will mean a difference of $10,000 every month.

In this hypothetical example, every percentage point is worth $1,000. However, even more importantly, the longer a donor sticks with a monthly giving program, the more likely it is that the donor will *continue* giving. Thus, you'll lose much more than one month's income with each lapsed donor.

In my experience, three elements *might* increase your fulfillment rate:

- *Inserts*—Good and appropriate inserts that motivate donors will boost response. Look for ones that you can use more than once. For instance: project updates, recipe cards, stories of people the donor helps, pictures, newspaper clippings, etc.

- *Outer envelopes*—You have to get them opened to get donors to reply. Test copy such as "Monthly Reminder," the name of the club, "January Pledge Reminder." You can also test colors, postage, and closed-face versus window envelopes.

- *Statement copy*—If you can make it relevant to the members, you enhance your income. You need to include a computer-generated personal reminder message on a donor's statement, and make it different each month. Here are a few examples:

  - *"Thanks for being up-to-date on your monthly pledge. It helps us to better plan our work in the fight against water pollution in Las Vegas."*

- *"Good friends like you are so valuable to a child with diabetes! Please take a moment to let us know that you are still a friend, and renew your support for diabetes research today."*
- *"Thank you so much for your commitment to the Vancouver AIDS Hospice. Your support means that many individuals will now be able to live their last days with <u>dignity</u>. That's a great gift!"*

How to raise even more money from your monthly donors

Monthly giving club members are likely to give you far more money than most other donors—over and above their monthly gifts. They'll make special gifts, buy your products, come to special events, and include your organization in their wills. And they'll do so in much higher proportions than the rest of your donors. However, *don't get greedy!* Too much pressure, too many Asks, all for the sake of an extra few dollars here or there, could lose you a lifetime of giving.

Apart from legacy gifts, the easiest and most logical of all the ways to increase your income from monthly donors dramatically is through *upgrading* them.

Let's say 1,000 people are currently active in your monthly giving program. You contact them by mail or by phone and 25 percent of them upgrade at an average of $5 a month. You can see from the table on page 159 what impact this has on your program.

For instance, if your 1,000 members each give you $10 a month on average and 25 percent of them upgrade their gifts by $5 per month, that translates into $1,250 per month, or $15,000 a year, more for your organization—year after year.

250 donors at a $5 increase = $1,250 month x 12 months = $15,000

Before that upgrade, the 1,000 donors would give an annual total of $120,000. An upgrade of $15,000 per year amounts to an increase of 12.5 percent for your annual monthly donor income!

Does 25 percent strike you as unrealistically high? I've taken part in upgrade programs that have persuaded 40 percent of the donors to increase their monthly gifts!

If you phone your monthly donors, you'll usually be more successful at upgrading, but it's a good idea to test phone versus mail.

DEFENDERS CLUB MEMBER

SPECIAL UPGRADE RESPONSE FORM

TO   Greg McDade, Executive Director, Sierra Legal Defence Fund

FROM   Gena Doe
1243 Elm Street
Anytown, ST 02938

SPEI003* (MU1)

Special Note   Greg, I realize that my donation of $20.00 is an effective way to bolster Sierra Legal's Longer term struggles to protect the environment. I want to do whatever I can to help so I am agreeing to <u>increase</u> my monthly contribution by:

- ☐ **$5** per month to a total amount of $25.00
- ☐ **$7** per month to a total amount of $27.00
- ☐ **$10** per month to a total amount of $30.00
- ☐ **$15** per month to a total amount of $35.00
- ☐ **$20** per month to a total amount of $40.00
- ☐ $Other _____

I understand that my my contribution increase will take effect immediately. I understand that I can change or cancel my membership at any time by calling our Vancouver office. I also understand that I will receive a charitable receipt at the end of the year for my entire years accumulated contributions.

_____   _____
SIGNATURE   DATE

SIERRA LEGAL DEFENCE FUND
#214-131 Water Street, Vancouver B.C. V6B 4M3 • 604-685-5618

A monthly donor upgrade promotion
Illustration 12.2

The outcome of an upgrade effort will depend on how your donors feel about your organization, what kind of calls they get, and what kind of packages they receive.

In an upgrade letter, emphasize the *cost per day* rather than the actual amount of the monthly increase. For example, if you're asking for a $5 upgrade, that's only 16 or 17 cents a day! When you put it that way, you make it easier for donors to say Yes.

An upgrade letter should be one or two pages long. It must include a thank-you, restate the case for monthly giving, note the impact the gifts achieve, and ask the donor to consider upgrading. It's important to state that even if a donor can't upgrade, you want her to know how much you appreciate her loyalty and commitment to your cause.

Impact of Annual Upgrades

	Before upgrade	After upgrade
Number of donors	1,000	1,000
Average monthly gift	$10	$11.25
Total monthly donor annual giving	$120,000	$135,000
Percentage of file upgrading	--	25%
Number of donors upgrading	--	250
Average monthly upgrade	--	$5
Monthly income increase	--	$1,250
Yearly income increase	--	$15,000
Percentage growth in annual income	--	12.5%

Annual upgrades of this amount are realistic for many organizations

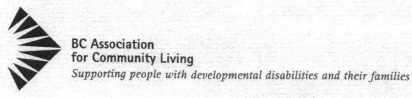

**BC Association
for Community Living**

Supporting people with developmental disabilities and their families

February 2, 1998

Mr. Harvey McKinnon
504 East 47th Ave.
Vancouver, B.C.
V5R 1N7

Dear Mr. McKinnon,

About six weeks ago I sent you your Circle of Friends certificate along with a request to consider increasing your monthly gift.

I'm sending you this brief note in case my letter failed to reach you given the postal strike. Or perhaps you set aside, but with the rush of the holiday season it slipped your mind. Since I've had this happen to me, I know how easy it is to plan to do something and then life takes over.

As I said then, BCACL's strongest supporters are Circle of Friends members like you. Your special commitment allows us to respond quickly and effectively to the needs of people with developmental disabilities.

So please consider this letter a gentle reminder. If you could increase your monthly pledge by $5 a month (that's 17 cents a day) or by any amount, you'll improve the lives of many people.

I realize this may be a sacrifice for you, but your decision will give the opportunity to serve more people in need of support.

I look forward to your decision and I thank you again for your extraordinary commitment to caring for others.

Yours sincerely,

Judy Carter-Smith
Executive Director

P.S.   Whatever you decide, please remember that our Circle of Friends membership means a tremendous amount to people with developmental disabilities. You make their lives more meaningful and healthy. And I want you to know I truly appreciate your concern and your generosity.

1

300 - 30 East 6th Avenue   TEL   604-875-1119   WEB www.vcn.bc.ca/bcacl   A UNITED WAY
Vancouver BC V5T 4P4   FAX   604-875-6744   E.MAIL info@bcacl.org   MEMBER AGENCY

This reminder upgrade request was very effective
Illustration 12.3

How many times should you ask for an upgrade?

I recommend an annual upgrade mailing. It's worthwhile starting anytime after a monthly donor has been enrolled in the program for at least ten months.

An upgrade campaign could consist of as little as a single letter, or it could include some combination of direct mail and telemarketing, perhaps involving multiple letters. The approach you take will depend on the kind of organization you work for and what you feel comfortable with. A number of my clients send a letter and then a reminder letter, or occasionally a letter, then a call.

Some clients simply phone to ask their donors to upgrade. This, too, has proven to be very profitable. It's all a matter of what you feel comfortable with and which approach is more cost-effective for your cause.

Another way to upgrade donors is through an automatic annual increase. Oxfam-Canada used this successfully in the early 1980s when inflation was high. We put a box on our monthly donor sign-up sheets called "Inflation Guard." The donor could check it off "to protect your donation." (Ten to 20 percent chose to do so.)

Back in the early 80s, I signed up a friend for a monthly giving program at $100 per month. She checked off the ten percent inflation guard. By the time inflation had dropped to two percent, she was giving nearly $200 a month!

As I write, inflation is extremely low, so this wouldn't work as well. It's possible, of course, to test, say, an automatic increase of ten percent each year. But I strongly suspect that a properly crafted upgrade appeal will be more profitable.

Once an individual has upgraded his monthly gift, I suggest asking him to increase the gift again the following year. This is less problematic with Electronic Funds Transfer and credit card giving: Even if he's slightly offended, it's unlikely that he'll take the initiative to drop out of the program. But be especially careful with monthly statement donors!

Setting higher giving club levels

At the outset, you have essentially three choices in a monthly giving club:

- An open-ended club people may join with monthly gifts of whatever amount they want.
- A club in which the monthly amount is fixed.

- Different levels of giving in the club. At, say, $10 a month, a donor receives certain basic benefits. At $25 a month, she receives greater benefits. (The two levels might even be defined as separate clubs, with different names.)

Naming the higher giving-level clubs makes it easier to upgrade new members by significant amounts. Major donor clubs at universities, hospitals, and other large institutions have proven that this sort of upgrading can work extremely well. There's no reason that any organization with a monthly donor club can't do the same.

Take the Council of Canadians, for example. Their lower-level monthly giving program is called the Canada Plan. In a higher-level club (The Citizen's Agenda Fund), the entry level is $500 per year, and donors are invited to give up to $10,000. The Council offers donors four giving options:

- Pay the full amount at once by check.
- Pay the full amount by Visa or MasterCard.
- Give by EFT ("automatic monthly deductions").
- Give the amount monthly by credit card.

Their lower-dollar monthly donors are invited to upgrade and are offered special club benefits: a hand-signed poster by noted Canadian wildlife artist Robert Bateman, an exclusive club newsletter, special reports, and invitations to advisory meetings.

Find your lost donors!

Monthly donors may disappear. Approximately one out of five individuals moves every year in North America. This means that unless you're communicating with your donors via first class mail—the kind of mail that will be returned if it isn't delivered—you'll lose touch with a certain number of them. (This is another good reason to collect your monthly donors' phone numbers!)

One common reason that a monthly EFT donor lapses is that she's closed her bank account and forgotten to notify your organization. She's very likely to rejoin when you contact her. (The sooner the better!)

Some of my clients' monthly donors are predominantly over 65. In other organizations, they're mostly between 35 and 55. The drop-out reasons vary, but the younger group is prone to more frequent moves, while the older group is prone to disability and death. (Death is nature's way of telling you that you only have to make one more monthly EFT payment.)

If you completely lose track of a donor, contact her financial institution. Tell them you have a tax receipt for the donor. You should have enough details already on file to identify the client to a bank's satisfaction. Often, banks will forward a receipt to a donor with a note asking for updated address information. If you're lucky, the bank will even include one of your BREs and a note citing the toll-free number donors may use to contact you directly. However, the ideal return envelope will feature a live stamp and a personally handwritten line in blue ink that reads, "Attention: Melanie" (the name of the person signing the letter asking for updated address information).

Getting that extra gift—an opportunity waiting

Will monthly donors give extra gifts? As already suggested, the answer is Yes.

There are two ways that this can happen. One, you give statement donors the option of making an "extra gift" in any month. You could, for instance, ask them to consider doubling their December gift. A certain percentage of donors in your file will do so.

The second, far more successful, method occurs with donors on credit cards and EFT. They are highly predisposed to extra giving. At Oxfam-Canada we discovered that 40 percent of EFT donors gave an extra gift during one year. A charity like Oxfam has an "advantage" because almost every year there's a special international emergency. Therefore these donors are undoubtedly more predisposed than those at your average charity. However, you can ask your donors if they would like your fundraising letters. You do this by saying, "While I realize that you make an incredibly generous commitment to our organization, I want to give you the option of receiving all our mail to find out what campaigns we're involved with."

Many of the donors who get this mail will send an extra gift or two during the year. EFT and credit cards are "unconscious" giving. Therefore, all the reasons that motivated a first gift and monthly donation in the first place will come into play as they read your latest appeal letter. EFT is so easy it hardly seems like giving, so I invariably give extra gifts to the causes I support.

Another option is to send a special year-end appeal to credit card and EFT donors. Again, you need a compelling case as to why an extra gift is important. You must ensure that an appeal for an extra gift does not conflict with your upgrade request, which is far more valuable. You may find that

September is a good time for a special letter to these special donors, or if you do your upgrades in February or March, then November would be a good time to appeal to them for an extra single gift. Make sure there's at least a two-month gap between the extra gift appeal and an upgrade.

Using special events

Another way to raise money from members is to invite them to your special events. You can invite your monthly donors to a general fundraising event where donors pay to attend or to a get-acquainted, meet-the-organization special event. The first is designed as a fundraiser. And you invite your monthly donors as a group. The event could be anything from a gala ball to a bowl-a-thon. For the get-acquainted event, you invite your monthly donors to a special dinner, or an open house, to meet the staff, ask questions, find out more about you, and build that important personal connection. This pays off handsomely in the long term.

Assuming you try to get donors to an event, you need a sense of who's on your database and what kind of demographic and psychographic profile they have. For instance, if many of your monthly donors are older females, they may not want to go out at night because they are afraid, or their night vision is poor. Understanding who they are helps you determine if and when they may come to your special events. Although most members will not attend, it makes people feel good to be asked. Just inviting them will help you build a stronger relationship.

For one of my clients, the David Suzuki Foundation, we often invite monthly donors to David's public speaking events. His show, "The Nature of Things," runs in 24 countries. Although the program has run on PBS, Discovery Channel, and A&E, he's not especially well known in the U.S., outside of Hollywood. But in Canada and Australia, he is a household name. As a result, when he does public presentations on the environment, he can sell out 1,000-seat halls.

If we have sufficient time, we send special invitations to major and monthly donors when he speaks in their areas. This works well. People will come up to David to tell him they are a Friend of the Foundation (the Foundation's monthly donor club), that they're happy to make an ongoing commitment and appreciative of the opportunity to meet David personally.

Selling products to your donors

You can look at your donors as simply donors or you can look at them from a marketing perspective. With a marketing viewpoint, you will raise

I GET THE PICTURE - $30 monthly is needed for some, up to $100 for others.

Dear Dr. Bob,

❏ **Yes!** I want to begin supporting a missionary overseas. Enclosed is my first gift of $_____ per month. Please send name and photo of the one assigned to me.

❏ Although I am not able to provide for a missionary every month, I want to help those who have no support at all. Enclosed is $_____ for missionaries on the foriegn field.

❏ I realize that Christian Aid also has needs and expenses. Enclosed is $_____ to help supply needs of the work.

    All gifts are tax deductible. Send to:

If needed, please correct your name and address on the reverse side.

**Christian Aid Mission
3045 Ivy Road
Charlottesville, Va 22903**

Native missionaries live simply and sacrificially.

43-303

Response device and outer envelope from a
monthly giving upgrade package
Illustration 12.4

more money and better satisfy your donors' needs and aspirations.

A nonprofit with even a small database of a few thousand donors can begin to develop cross-marketing opportunities. These are ways to "sell" new products to your donors. In fact, monthly giving and planned giving are just two examples of additional ways in which a donor becomes involved with your cause.

A major U.K. nonprofit discovered that donors who bought into any part of their program were more likely to buy into another part. This is logical. But what is important is that once they bought into a second part they became much better donors.

For example, the nonprofit has a mail order catalog. As one might expect, the most likely buyers of catalog products are donors. And they found that when donors bought catalog products, they became far more generous donors. This means developing appropriate product lines that will interest your donors. You should make money on the initial sale; and the extra donations are a bonus. For monthly donors, this could be a way to build loyalty and therefore get them to increase their pledge amount.

Museums, public television stations, international development agencies, and other charities often sell to their donors via catalogs, stores, or other methods.

Your monthly donors are among the most likely market for these products because they have such a strong affiliation with your organization. For this reason, you might consider selling something if you have a large monthly donor program of potential buyers.

One of the most profitable products is holiday greeting cards. If you can print them in volume, you should make a profit of at least 300 percent. They also serve to promote your organization to the people they're mailed to—often the friends of your best donors, who are likely to have similar giving tendencies.

Needless to say, you probably also want to offer these products to your regular donor list, which can increase your profits by amortizing production costs.

Before I would do this for any organization, however, I would analyze the donor base, do some research, and test a small number of products to see if it would be profitable. Other key questions to ask are:

- Do you have the capability of fulfilling orders efficiently?
- Can you deal with production, returns, and various other areas?
- Is this a profitable way to spend staff time?

Providing a service to your monthly donors

Consider what services you can offer to your donors. For instance, estate planning seminars provide a service to your donors. Other membership benefits could include a toll-free number where they can receive free information on health issues, protecting the environment, or animal nutrition. The list is long, and these materials should be benefit-focused and educational.

When donors ask for information, they tell you what interests them. This is worth loading into your database as long as you can use it. By offering services to monthly donors, you can enhance your relationship with them.

Reactivating lapsed monthly donors

When an individual drops out of your monthly giving club—especially if it's for economic reasons, such as retirement—I suggest you write him a thank-you letter:

- Tell him how much you appreciate his tremendous support over the years.

- Refer to his gift history, and acknowledge that his circumstances have changed.

- Tell him you're sorry he's unable to continue his membership.

- Given his long-term relationship with you, invite him to continue receiving your newsletter, so he'll know the money he's invested continues to be well spent. Enclose a reply form with copy like "If you no longer want to receive our newsletter, please let us know. We'll be happy to honor your request. Otherwise we will keep you on our mailing list with the hope that you gain some satisfaction and inspiration from hearing about the kind of work you've had a long history of supporting."

- Tell him you believe you still have a special relationship with him and would like it to continue. Emphasize that, "although we know you may not be able to contribute again, we just want to send this as a way of thanking you for your support over the years."

When you send such a letter, you accomplish three important things:

- First, some donors will re-evaluate their gift-giving priorities. A certain percentage of people stop their monthly gifts because their income has gone down. But this doesn't necessarily mean that they've stopped giving to all charities—merely that your organization hasn't made the cut in their priority-setting decisions.

- Secondly, it's a good investment. Sending someone a newsletter costs the organization next to nothing.

- Third, by sending these to former pledgers you create an opportunity to provide planned giving information. Many of those who drop out of monthly giving programs do so because they're retired. They're good prospects for planned gifts!

- Besides, someone who gets one of these letters may even inherit money later. The extra boost your letter provides may cause them to think of sharing that good fortune with you.

However, in addition to the potential financial benefits, letters of this sort will strengthen your relationships with long-time (perhaps life-long) donors: You demonstrate that you actually care about them and their past giving, and that you're not just concerned about future gifts. (That's important to emphasize.)

This is the kind of letter that people will talk about with their friends—people who may decide to give to you.

Exchanging or renting monthly donor names

You may feel uncomfortable about exchanging your monthly donor names. However, the benefits can be enormous. Only three to ten percent of donors on most lists will ever become monthly donors. So, when you use another organization's monthly donor list, you get access to the cream of the crop. And remember, your donors are highly committed to you so you are unlikely to lose any as a result of the exchange, especially if they give electronically.

If you exchange your monthly donors for another nonprofit's monthly donors, you have a choice of offers to make to the prospects:

- Ask them to join your monthly donor program, because they are already familiar with the concept.

- Ask for just a single gift.

- Have a monthly donor focus with a single gift option.

- Have a single-gift focus with a monthly donor option.

My strong feeling is that your offer should focus on the single-gift with a monthly donor option.

Your ultimate goal is to convert them to monthly giving, but first you want to acquire as many names as possible for your mailing list. You are far better off asking for a single gift than a monthly commitment. In other words, people on this list are prime targets for a monthly donor program—and the volume of new names is what is important. That said, I always believe you should soft-sell a monthly donor program when you prospect for single gifts.

If you've already asked your monthly donors if they don't mind being traded, you can use this select list to trade with other organizations. But only trade for their monthly donors and only trade with organizations with comparable donors and monthly gift amounts.

If you have your donors' permission to trade their names and if there's no resulting drop-off, this kind of trading can be incredibly lucrative. After all, you are appealing to prospects who have already demonstrated their willingness to make a monthly pledge. Since they are probably among the top ten percent of donors for most organizations, it's a great list. Code the respondents as prospects with a propensity for monthly giving, and then follow up with appropriate invitations.

Should you rent your monthly donor list? Organizations, especially those with thousands of donors in their monthly donor program, could make a fair bit of money from list rental. My advice is: *Don't do it.*

Even if you rent 10,000 names at $100 per thousand and make $1,000, losing even a single donor out of the 10,000 will cost you more than you make. If enough donors find out that your rent out their names—and they will—some will quit.

Monthly donors—your best opportunity for a legacy

There is no other group on your donor file more likely to leave you money in their wills than your monthly donors. These are donors who have really bonded with your cause. They're willing to give you direct access to their personal bank account numbers, and to make an ongoing, multi-year commitment. Organizations that have long-running programs find that their monthly donors are by far the most likely to make planned gifts.

Gwen Chapman, past director of membership and marketing for the World Wildlife Fund of Canada, says, "We have found that these donors are more loyal." She adds, "Many have committed to planned gifts as well." This is also my experience with a number of causes.

Share *Plan*

November 12, 1991

Mr. Harvey MacKinnon

Sharon Norman
SharePlan Coordinator

1011 Bloor Street West
Toronto, Ontario
M6H 1M1

Toronto: 416-535-6767
Toll-free: 1-800-387-4760

Charitable registration
number: 0221135-03

Dear Harvey,

As you may already know, OXFAM-Canada, with the six
other OXFAMs around the world, has just launched its 50th
Anniversary Year Campaign. This campaign, called Working
for Change, is a celebration of our partners overseas, and
of their efforts to improve their lives. It is also an
opportunity for us to inform more people about our work and
our hopes for a better world.

This will be a year of special outreach to strengthen
the Oxfam movement worldwide. We hope that by the end of
the year at least one million people will have signed our
enclosed International Resolution card and pledged to join
us in working for a fairer world.

At the same time we are inviting current supporters to
make a special 50th Anniversary gift to Oxfam. There was
some debate about whether we ought to invite you, as a
SharePlan donor, to make such a gift, because you already
do your share, and more than your share! But ultimately,
we felt we should invite you to become involved.

Already a number of SharePlan donors have agreed to
serve as ambassadors to the general public this year.
People like Muriel Duckworth from Halifax, (recent Pearson
Peace Medal Prize winner) and Sonja Smits, (from CBC's
Street Legal) have signed the resolution card and said they
would be happy to do what they could to help. They have
given special anniversary gifts as well!

We would be delighted if you too would be able to give
an extra gift this year. A special contribution of $25,
$50, or whatever amount you could afford, would mean we
could do much more for those people who need our support.

I hope that you decide to become involved in the
campaign, but whatever you decide, thank you most sincerely
for your ongoing commitment and support through SharePlan.

Yours sincerely,

Sharon Norman
SharePlan Coordinator

🌐 **WORKING FOR CHANGE**
50TH ANNIVERSARY CAMPAIGN

Printed on
recycled paper.

A special one-time gift appeal to monthly EFT donors
Illustration 12.5

Extensive research has shown that the people who leave you bequests are not necessarily the wealthiest people on your donor file. Instead, legacy donors tend to be loyal, low-level donors who have given regularly for many years. This is exactly the kind of donor who joins your monthly donor program.

Legacy donors are interested in developing a personal relationship with a charitable organization. People who give on a monthly basis and who are members of a special club certainly fit this profile.

You are probably familiar with the estimates that about $13 trillion in the U.S. ($1 trillion in Canada) will be transferred over the next 15 years to the next generation. Nonprofits deserve a share of this money. This is the greatest wealth transfer in history, and if charities receive even three percent of this money, it will be a phenomenal windfall.

Monthly donors are among your best prospects. According to many planned giving experts, a donor who has given $25 a year for ten years is a more likely prospect than a donor who has given one or two large gifts over ten years. The ten-year commitment shows that the donor is serious about your cause—and may support your organization with his or her final gift.

You should always keep in touch with lapsed monthly donors who contributed for a number of years. When people retire, their annual giving often declines due to a decreased cash flow. This does not mean that their commitment has stopped—far from it. But it could mean your organization will need to wait a few years before the donor can make another gift—or the ultimate one. If you lose touch, they may decide to give part of their estate to other nonprofits. Ask these individuals if they would like to continue receiving information, or simply send newsletters and other information as appropriate.

Don't mail them twelve fundraising letters a year for ten years, but consider communicating with these donors once a year with an appeal, an invitation to rejoin the program, or your newsletter. All you need is a couple of legacies from this group to cover the costs of mailing to these lapsed donors—unless you have a couple hundred thousand lapsed monthly donors!

Legacy marketing, like monthly donor program promotion, has to be repetitive and continuous. You never know what combination of circumstances and timing will motivate a donor to leave you a legacy or pledge a monthly commitment. An emotional tie to your organization is essential for people deciding which organization to bequeath a legacy.

Send a special letter to your monthly donors to invite them to join your legacy society. (They've already proven they are "joiners.") Legacy societies are important because many people like joining clubs where they share interests and goals with other members. Legacy societies also allow your organization to recognize members' special contributions in a variety of ways.

Identifying the ages of your monthly donors is very important. We know that people in their 60s, and sometimes even in their early 70s, aren't all that eager to talk about what happens after they die. Then as people reach their later 70s and beyond, they accept that it's a matter of when they die, not if they die. They've generally moved past the denial phase and realize they won't live forever.

In the United States, you can buy age-overlays for your file at quite a reasonable cost from a number of vendors. You can find these vendors at conferences of the National Society of Fund Raising Executives (NSFRE) or in most fundraising publications.

And there's more

Just in case you're still not convinced that monthly donors are worth a lot more than most occasional donors, I'll tell you a story about one New York-based nonprofit.

Their development director met face-to-face with a $100-per-month credit card sustainer. The outcome of the meeting? The donor decided to give *$15,000 per quarter* in addition to his $100 per month. Over a year, this was the equivalent of an additional $5,000 a month. A pretty good upgrade!

CHAPTER 13
Long-Term Value: How much is a monthly donor really worth?

Though the thought of mathematical calculations may make your left eye start twitching, you have no choice. A certain amount of number-crunching is essential when you're building a monthly giving program. (You'll notice, however, that I've left this uncomfortable topic until the end of this book!)

There are three benchmarks you'll need to track. Let's look at each of them briefly.

Cost Per Response (CPR)

The CPR consists of two components: (a) the front-end cost, which is the cost to acquire a monthly donor (including such elements as the cost of a space ad or a direct mail campaign), and (b) the back end, which includes all subsequent costs (including any premiums used) to thank and welcome a member of a monthly giving club. The CPR is the sum of all these front-end and back-end costs, divided by the number of responses to the recruitment campaign. (Is your eye twitching yet?) Some people define CPR as just the front-end cost. I feel that including the back-end cost gives you a more accurate picture of your real cost per response.

Long-Term Value (LTV)

The Long-Term Value (LTV) is an estimate of the total net income generated by one average donor over his complete giving history. This would include—in addition to monthly gifts—any special gifts, profits on product sales, and any other net revenue your organization might realize from a donor.

LTV projections are made on the basis of past and current donor behavior as well as educated guesswork about the impact of any new programs and strategies you implement.

Return On Investment (ROI)

There are a number of ways to calculate ROI. Here's a simple formula that I like which calcultes ROI over a lifetime, whereas many traditional businesses calculate ROI over a fiscal year.

ROI is calculated by subtracting the total of front-end acquisition costs and all back-end cultivation and servicing costs from the Long-Term Value, and dividing the resulting figure by the acquisition cost. In other words, you divide the net revenue you'll derive from a donor by the net investment you've made in acquiring that donor. As a formula, it looks like this:

$$ROI = (LTV - \text{acquisition cost} - \text{cultivation cost})/\text{acquisition cost}$$

Straightforward enough? No? Let's examine a couple of examples of ROI before we return to CPR (cost per response) and LTV (long-term value).

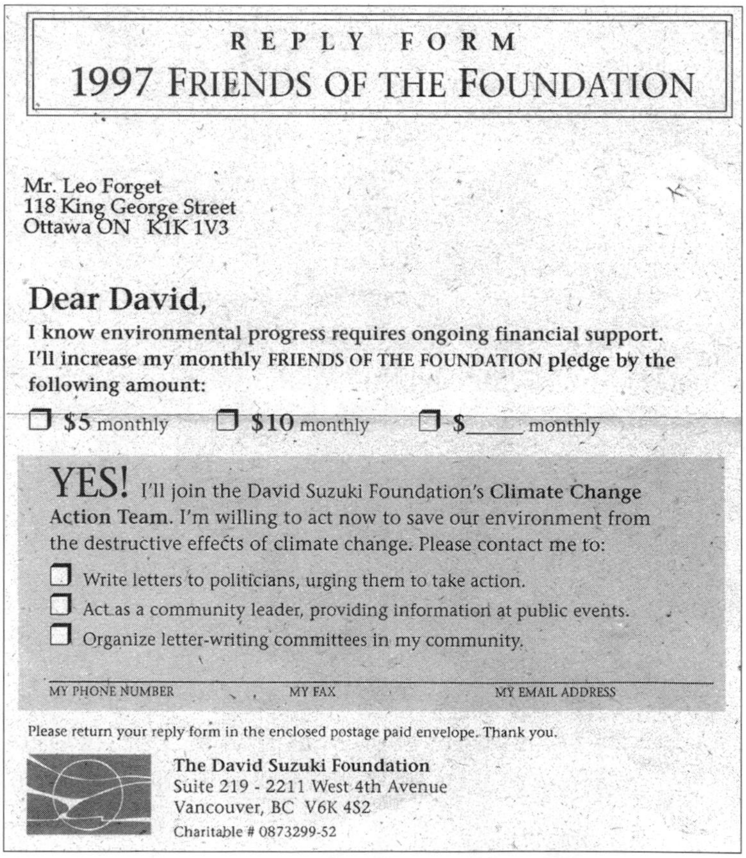

REPLY FORM

1997 FRIENDS OF THE FOUNDATION

Mr. Leo Forget
118 King George Street
Ottawa ON K1K 1V3

Dear David,

I know environmental progress requires ongoing financial support. I'll increase my monthly FRIENDS OF THE FOUNDATION pledge by the following amount:

❒ $5 monthly ❒ $10 monthly ❒ $_____ monthly

YES! I'll join the David Suzuki Foundation's **Climate Change Action Team.** I'm willing to act now to save our environment from the destructive effects of climate change. Please contact me to:

❒ Write letters to politicians, urging them to take action.
❒ Act as a community leader, providing information at public events.
❒ Organize letter-writing committees in my community.

MY PHONE NUMBER MY FAX MY EMAIL ADDRESS

Please return your reply form in the enclosed postage paid envelope. Thank you.

The David Suzuki Foundation
Suite 219 - 2211 West 4th Avenue
Vancouver, BC V6K 4S2
Charitable # 0873299-52

Reply form from a monthly giving upgrade letter
Illustration 13.1

ROI: Example A

In a telemarketing campaign, the average cost of recruiting each monthly donor is $55. Cultivation and resolicitation costs (all subsequent costs over years of giving) add another $100. You estimate the Long-Term Value of the average monthly donor's giving to be $1,255.

To compute the ROI, simply subtract that $155 in acquisition and cultivation costs from the Long-Term Value. You get $1,100 Net. Then divide the result by that same $55 acquisition cost:

$$ROI = (\$1{,}255 - \$55) - \$100 = \$1{,}100 \div \$55 = \$20 \; (or \; 2{,}000\%)$$

In other words, your telemarketing campaign has enabled you to recruit new monthly givers with a projected return of $20 for each $1 you invested in acquiring and servicing them.

ROI: Example B

The average Long-Term Value of a direct mail-acquired monthly donor is $2,800 to your organization. Front-end recruitment costs total approximately $100, with back-end cultivation and resoliciting costs adding another $100 ($200 total). Here, then, is how to calculate your Return on Investment:

$$\$2{,}800 - \$200 = \$2{,}600 \div \$100 \; (aquisition \; cost) = \$26 \; (or \; 2{,}600\%)$$

Your return on your investment is 26 times your cost.

It's vital to understand that ROI varies—sometimes dramatically—by the means of giving. It does you no good to lump all EFT, credit card, and check donors together. Typically, the average Long-Term Value of EFT donors is five to ten times that of statement donors—and EFT donors are usually more valuable than donors who pay by credit card.

If you don't currently track your donors and their giving over time, and project their performance over a lifetime of giving, start now. Every dollar you spend on fundraising should be viewed as an investment. To make cost-effective decisions, you need to be able to compare returns from different investments, donor file segments, and media lists. Otherwise, you're liable to make costly mistakes—and you're unlikely to maximize your income.

For instance, suppose a telemarketing campaign to recruit monthly donors results in an ROI of 2 in the first year alone—$2 for every $1 invested. Your direct mail campaign yields an ROI in the first year of just $1.50 per $1 invested. Since the telemarketing program brought in 33 percent more money than direct mail, you might decide to switch all your prospect recruitment budget into telemarketing.

Aha! Now suppose that, after four years, you lose 60 percent of the telemarketing-recruited monthly donors. The attrition rate for your direct mail-sourced monthly giving club members is only 25 percent.

Assuming that the average monthly gifts for the two groups are similar, the LTV of the direct mail names would then be far greater—and at this far lower rate of attrition, maybe ultimately four times more valuable!

You'll only know what really has value when you use measurement tools that can show you how and where to invest your scarce dollars.

Cost per response (CPR)

Back to CPR.

There are two kinds of CPR (not counting the kind you'll need if you keep smoking).

Depending on your promotional objectives, you might look for two kinds of responses: either leads (generated, for example, by a 30-second TV spot), or actual sign-ups ("orders" or "sales" in the lingo of commercial direct marketing). If you're generating leads which you attempt to convert into donors, your ROI calculations are a bit more complex, because you also need to know your conversion rate and cost per conversion.

Stay with me, please. This isn't as bad as it seems.

Let's say your objective is to generate leads and convert them later into monthly donors. Your total acquisition cost for a monthly donor includes the following elements:

- the net cost of generating leads

- the conversion rate (the percentage of leads who are converted into monthly donors: e.g., if you generate 500 leads and convert 125 to monthly giving, your conversion rate is 25 percent)

- the cost of converting leads into monthly donors

At the same time, there is generally some offsetting income. For example, lead-generation programs may yield one-time gifts—sometimes lots of them. So may lead-conversion efforts. All this additional single-gift income may be subtracted from the gross acquisition cost to calculate the net acquisition cost. (Now, to be a stickler for accuracy, you'll also need to take into account the fact that some of these single-gift donors may eventually become monthly donors. This phenomenon needs to be tracked, since it also affects the economics of your monthly giving program. But let's stick to a less complicated example, for the time being.)

Say you spend $30,000 on a mailing to 50,000 prospective monthly donors. The response consists of two components: 500 leads (people who ask for information about the monthly giving program) and a total of $20,000 in one-time gifts (much of it, though not all, from some of the 500 leads). So the net cost of acquiring those 500 leads is:

$$\$30,000 - \$20,000, \text{ or } \$10,000 \div 500 = \$20 \text{ cost per lead}$$

If the conversion rate for the 500 leads is 25 percent, you'll acquire 125 monthly donors. Let's assume the conversion costs total about $2 per lead, or $1,000. In effect, then, you've spent a total of $11,000 to acquire 125 new monthly giving club members ($10,000 + $1,000). So the CPR in this program—the average acquisition cost of each new member—is:

$$CPR = \$11,000 \div 125 \text{ members} = \$88$$

If you add $2 to thank each member, you get a $90 CPR.

The spin-off effects of monthly giving

A monthly giving program enhances the Long-Term Value of all your donors. It's important to understand how and why.

Let's say you calculate the LTV for your average single-gift donor at $180. Say it costs you $20 to acquire a new donor, and another $40 to service that donor during her lifetime of giving to your organization. Your ROI, then, is as follows:

$$ROI = (\$180 - \$20 - \$40) \ \$120 \div \$20 = \$6 \ (or \ 600\%)$$

In this case, 1,000 single-gift donors will have an LTV of $180,000 (1,000 x $180).

Now, say that five percent of these donors, or 50 people, reply to your regular house letters (no extra cost) and join your new monthly giving club. If each gives $10 per month for seven years—a realistic estimate if they enroll in EFT—those 50 people are "worth" $840 each ($10 x 12 x 7). Their giving would total $42,000 (50 x $840)—let's say with an additional $2,000 in costs—so your net is $40,000. This will increase the overall LTV of those original 1,000 donors.

We've already calculated that value as $180,000. But, for simplicity, let's deduct the single gifts those 50 monthly donors would otherwise have given in the six subsequent years. Call that one $30 gift/donor/year. That represents $9,000 (50 x 6 x $30). Subtract this amount from $180,000, leaving $171,000. That's the approximate LTV of the 950 donors who did not become monthly givers.

But now you may add the $40,000 LTV of the 50 monthly donors. That yields a total of $211,000 ($171,000 + $40,000). If you divide that by the total number of donors, 1,000, you find that the LTV of all 1,000 donors has jumped to $213 on average ($213,000/1,000). That's 17.2 percent more income.

There is, of course, a corresponding rise in your ROI:

$$(\$211 - \$20 - \$40) = \$151 \div \$20 = \$7.55 \ (or \ 755\%)$$

In other words, by increasing the Long-Term Value of your donors with a monthly giving program, you can now afford to invest more money in acquiring new donors!

These are important calculations to make, but be careful about averages. Some will perform better than others. You want to know the CPR, LTV, and ROI for each donor file segment, each list, television show, video, mailing, phone campaign, and so forth. Averages can often hide valuable information. As you acquire more details, you can focus on the most profitable areas. You can also test to improve the marginal areas and increase your return from successful ones.

A client of mine recently conducted a monthly giving club recruitment campaign via telemarketing in which the single-gift income covered all the phone costs. So the new monthly donors were pure profit from Day One!

Remember: LTV is only an estimate, and a rough one at that. Naturally, you project LTV with the best information and finest analytical skills at your disposal. But LTV can change. For instance, you might improve your

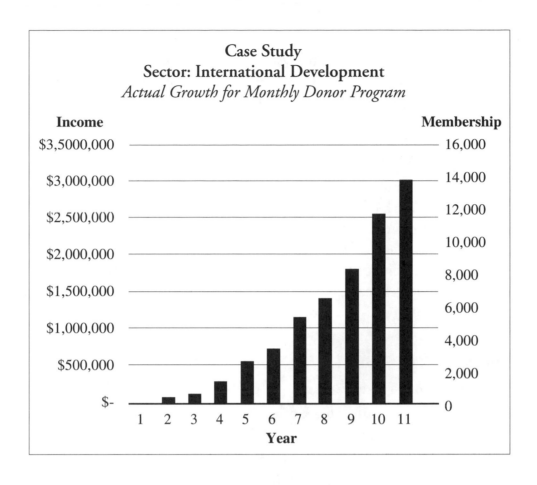

Case Study
Sector: International Development
Actual Growth for Monthly Donor Program

Year	Income	Memberships
1	$15,000	140
2	$53,000	500
3	$103,000	1,000
4	$306,000	2,000
5	$531,000	3,100
6	$705,000	4,100
7	$1,150,000	5,400
8	$1,400,000	6,500
9	$1,730,000	8,000
10	$2,520,000	11,700
11	$3,007,000	13,900

donor loyalty policies, and instead of a five-year average lifetime of giving, you might retain donors for ten years on average. Or an aggressive campaign to convert statement donors to EFT might boost the program's value overnight. (Conversely, your executive director could be caught with her hand in the organization's till. This could raise serious questions about what were once valid projections!)

In any event, these are simplistic ways to calculate value. To learn more, check your local university or college for marketing and economics courses that will give you far more analytical and sophisticated tools to use. The Direct Marketing Association in New York runs seminars across the U.S. in marketing math and finance. And companies that specialize in Long-Term Value analysis often advertise in major fundraising publications. Remember that even if these calculations seem daunting, don't let them deter you from starting or building a program!

Evaluate ROI, CPR, and LTV by source

Many factors may affect Long-Term Value:

- Certain lists outperform others (so you can't simply compare direct mail versus telemarketing; you have to go deeper in your analysis).

- Seasonality, too, may affect Long-Term Value: Donors recruited in non-peak seasons tend to have a higher Long-Term Value (even though they may cost more to recruit).

- Donors recruited with a special premium may stop giving sooner than those recruited without a premium.

- Monthly donors are more likely to leave bequests. You may not include this factor in your LTV calculations, unless you have an active, ongoing planned giving program and some data to manipulate. But it's important to know that legacies are far more likely to come from these incredibly loyal monthly donors.

- A respondent to a space ad, especially one who replies by mail, may have a higher LTV than a donor acquired through some other means. (This may be because such an individual is more thoughtful about his decisions. He must write down and then call your 800 number or write and mail a request for information.)

Calculating Return On Investment and Long-Term Value
for monthly donors

To calculate an accurate ROI for the members of your monthly giving program, you must know the following:

- the cost of each type of recruitment

- the original recruitment method for each club member

- the rate of member lapsing by recruitment source

- upgrades (percentages and actual dollars) by recruitment source

- the total income from these monthly donors

- other costs

Ideally, each of the above calculations needs to be made for each method of payment, since an EFT donor may be worth eight times as much as a check donor.

When looking at the costs of a monthly giving program, you generally don't include fixed costs and overhead, as this can distort the real return on investment. (Of course, you need to know what these are, anyway!)

Since you are calculating value over time, you may want to "discount" the dollars from future years, because of inflation. This gets complicated, because in times of high inflation, the dollar quickly drops in value. In times of low inflation, the difference in value is small. But you can select an arbitrary annual figure to discount LTV—perhaps five percent, or ten percent—to take into account inflation and other risks.

To do this all scientifically, it might be worthwhile to enlist the help of a database marketing specialist. These calculations pose a number of challenges. However the results can be dramatic. For instance, knowing your ROI will allow you to compare alternative investment opportunities. This might point the way to redirecting your recruitment efforts from, say, a door-to-door canvass into telemarketing.

When calculating Long-Term Value, be sure to deduct costs if the figure you're looking for is the net value per member during a lifetime of support. Include all your costs, both fixed and variable: design and copywriting, printing, space or time buys, production of your advertising, placement or mailing costs, deductions for EFT or credit card processing fees, thank-you phone calls, uploading information into your database, regular correspondence with donors, staff people to handle this part of the process, stop-payment costs, premiums, fulfillment costs, and anything else.

WORLD HOME BIBLE LEAGUE

Dennis M. Mulder, Executive Director • John F. DeVries, Director of International Ministries

September 30, 1987

RECEIVED

OCT 0 6 1987

Mr Mal Warwick
P O Box 1282
Berkeley, CA 94701

Dear Mal:

Please accept my personal thanks for your recent and generous contribution to the World Home Bible League. Your help came at a very critical time.

We're thankful that God continues to prompt men, women, and children to seek Him. And what a joy it is to be part of the solution--providing hope and comfort to hurting, lonely, afraid people, through the placement of God's Word.

Our work would not be possible if it weren't for you, and many others like you across this great land of ours. That's why we're so thankful for your partnership.

World Home Bible League is committed to sharing God's Word wherever people seek it. . .in Asia, Africa, Latin America, and the Middle East. We believe the Bible is still the greatest missionary tool available.

That's why I hope you will accept my personal invitation to join a small, select group of League partners who have undertaken to help in this critical time when requests for Scriptures exceed our ability to respond.

This group, called the **WORLD MISSIONARY PASSBOOK MEMBERSHIP GROUP**, is made up of individuals who pledge a small amount each month--usually just $10 or $12 to help us meet the challenge of unfilled Scripture requests.

Since we can count on your monthly plege gift--along with those from other World Missionary Passbook members-- the League can plan more efficiently. What's more, by pledging a small monthly gift, you are able to give more to the Lord's work through small, manageable amounts. As a result, we reach more people with God's Word, and that's what our work is all about.

Think of it. Your own pledge of $12 per month--only 40 cents a day, less than a cup of coffee--will allow the League each year to place 48 Bibles in the hands of desperately seeking men and women. Just imagine their gratefulness as your gifts make such events possible.

16801 Van Dam Road • South Holland, Illinois 60473 • (312)-331-2094
Outside Illinois • Toll Free • 1-(800)-334-7017

My Monthly Pledge Commitment To Join The
WORLD MISSIONARY PASSBOOK MEMBERSHIP GROUP

☑ Yes, please enroll me as a member of the League's WORLD MISSIONARY PASSBOOK MEMBERSHIP GROUP. I've indicated my monthly pledge commitment below. I understand I may cancel my pledge whenever I wish.

☐ $12   ☐ $10   ☐ $18   ☐ $_____

☐ I cannot make a monthly pledge at this time, however I will continue my support of the League with a one-time gift of $_____.

Mr. Mal Warwick
P. O. Box 1282
Berkeley, CA 94701

Partner Membership No.

World Home Bible League's
WORLD MISSIONARY PASSBOOK
MEMBERSHIP GROUP

Member
_____

Dennis M Mulder
Rev. Dennis M. Mulder
Executive Director

Please make your check payable to WORLD HOME BIBLE LEAGUE and return it along with this reply form.

World Home Bible League
South Holland, IL 60473

Combined donor thank-you and monthly giving
conversion package *(this page and next)*
Illustration 13.2

BUSINESS REPLY MAIL
FIRST CLASS   PERMIT NO. 51   SOUTH HOLLAND, IL

Postage will be paid by addressee

 World Home Bible League
South Holland, IL 60473

NO POSTAGE
NECESSARY
IF MAILED
IN THE
UNITED STATES

Page 2

We want people who love the lost and love God's Word to join us. I know your commitment to give a monthly contribution of $10, $12, or even $18 may mean some personal sacrifice on your part. I appreciate that fact very much, especially as I read my mail each week and learn how people struggle to make ends meet, yet faithfully meet their pledge promise.

All I can say to these folks, and to you, is "thank you," and I promise to use these gifts in the most efficient and effective way we know.

And the only thing I can give in return is the inner knowledge and satisfaction that comes from knowing that your partnership with World Home Bible League will change lives for eternity.

-- Men, women, and children who otherwise might never know about Jesus Christ wil learn of his grace and love

-- New Christians who want to know more about Christ will have study materials that will help them grow

-- Christians who have been waiting for years for their first Bible will now get one

All of these things will happen because you care enough to get involved.

You can step out from the crowd and take a stand today. I hope you will help us by making a small monthly pledge. With your continued help, we can meet the extraordinary challenges that lie ahead.

Please use the enclosed reply card to accept my invitation to become a member of the WORLD MISSIONARY PASSBOOK MEMBERSHIP GROUP.

Each month I'll send you a pledge reminder that will report on how your monthly gifts are helping to change the world for Jesus Christ.

Your partner in
sending God's Word,

Rev. Dennis M. Mulder
Executive Director

P.S. Your regular monthly pledge gifts can help us reach more people for Jesus Christ. If you can't make a monthly pledge commitment now, perhaps you'd show your continued support for Bible placement by making a special gift today. Thanks and God bless you.

(Including general overhead is optional. I advise not doing so.)

Pay special attention to the hard costs of servicing monthly donors: premiums, yearly mailing costs, credit card or EFT fees, and so forth. If it costs you $10 a year to service a $10 a month donor, that's one thing. If that same donor costs you $65 a year, there's a big difference! Your net income goes from $110 ($120 - $10) to $55 ($120 - $65). In other words, it drops in half.

Over the course of time

The value (and accuracy) of benchmarking grows over time. In fact, many of these calculations are simply out of the question unless you've got a sizable backlog of data about your donors and your fundraising costs and returns.

What you'll know after Year 1

In the first year of a monthly giving program, you can determine what arguments will convince your donors to sign up. You can calculate the sources through which you may most successfully recruit new donors, and the cost-effectiveness of each medium or method you use. You can also determine something about what your new donors have in common. And, if you test systematically throughout the year, you can discover the best time or times to make your first request.

What you'll know after Year 3

By the end of Year 3, you'll have statistics on the attrition rate for each form of giving (EFT, credit cards, checks). You'll be able to predict with fair accuracy how many of your monthly donors will upgrade, and for how much. You'll know which are the cost-effective recruitment methods. You'll be able to project how many people will join through phone campaigns and special appeal letters, by ads or articles in your newsletter, and by a standard direct mail invitation.

You'll know the best times to ask donors to join the monthly giving club. You'll know whether you can recruit people to join through prospect mailings without depressing overall response. You'll have discovered most of the bugs in the system and—with luck—eliminated them. You may now be able to dedicate a full-time staff person to serve the needs of your monthly donors.

What you'll know after Year 5, Year 10, and beyond

After five years, you'll have a strong sense of the Long-Term Value of a monthly donor. You'll know what the attrition graph will look like, and you can plot out what income you can expect from your members, based on the data you've collected.

By the end of the tenth year of your monthly giving program, you'll know what a new donor is worth—and you'll probably still have between 10 and 55 percent of the monthly donors you recruited ten years earlier. Many of these people will continue to give until they die. They're committed and predictable. They've probably been around longer than almost all your organization's staff and board members! They're truly dedicated to your mission. They will give serious consideration to remembering you in their wills. Very likely, many have already done so.

Monthly donors vs. Single-gift donors

If you haven't yet started a monthly giving program but want to do so — or, better yet, if you want to, but your boss or board are opposed—you'll find it very useful to look at the Long-Term Value of monthly donors as compared to that of single-gift donors. As you'll find, the differences result from donor loyalty and attrition.

Consider the following hypothetical example as a guide to estimating the value of your own organization's donors. Keep in mind that many variables affect this picture, and the estimates you derive will be approximate at best. However, if you do everything right, these estimates will prove to be conservative. Many groups do much better than this.

First let's take a look at the typical pattern of attrition of direct mail-acquired single-gift donors. Charities commonly calculate that 50 per cent of the people who make donations will never do so again, and, of those who do, some 60 to 80 percent will continue to renew annually in later years. This range depends on the size of your program, your cause, the quality of your direct mail and telemarketing programs, the economy, your profile, your staff, your competition, and a multitude of other factors. So, what do these numbers mean in practice?

As you can see in the accompanying chart (page 186), of 1,000 donors acquired in Year 1, 500 will remain active at the end of Year 2, having renewed their support in response to either a membership renewal notice or a special appeal in the course of the year. In subsequent years, let's assume—generously—a 70 percent renewal rate in Years 3, 4, and 5, with 80 percent in the next three years and 90 percent in the final three years of the decade.

In this fashion, the original cohort of 1,000 donors will wither away. Just 83 will remain on file at the end of Year 10.

Attrition of Direct Mail-Acquired Single-Gift Donors

Year	Renewal Rate	# Donors Remaining
1	50%	1,000
2	70%	500
3	70%	350
4	70%	245
5	80%	196
6	80%	157
7	80%	126
8	90%	113
9	90%	102
10	90%	92

Now consider the picture that emerges over a decade for 1,000 donors enrolled in an electronic-based monthly giving program. Here, the attrition rate is assumed to be ten percent per year.

Attrition of Direct Mail-Acquired Monthly Donors

Renewal Year	Rate	# Donors Remaining
1	90%	1,000
2	90%	900
3	90%	810
4	90%	729
5	90%	656
6	90%	590
7	90%	531
8	90%	478
9	90%	430
10	90%	387

Clearly, the difference is immense. For starters, you'll have 387 donors left at the end of the decade as opposed to 92. But that's just the beginning. Those 387 donors will have given twelve gifts per year—every year!

What accounts for such an enormous difference?

Loyalty.

The difference lies in your organization's commitment to building long-term relationships with your donors—and the loyal, continuing support they give you in return.

Attrition by method of giving

Despite your best efforts, however, you'll see attrition in your monthly donor file. The best you can do is minimize the losses.

The major factor affecting your rate of attrition is the percentage of donors in each of the three major giving streams: EFT, credit card, and check donors. Generally you can expect the rate of attrition to fall into the following ranges:

Method of Giving	Annual Attrition Rate
EFT	5 - 15%
Credit cards	10 - 25%
Paper checks	10 - 35%

All three methods are appealing by contrast with single-gift giving, especially when you consider that only 50 percent of first-time donors are likely to give again while the other 50 percent disappear into the ozone. The attrition rate is usually highest in the first year. If you're running a good program, in Year 1 you can expect to lose 30 percent of check donors, 15 percent of those who give by credit card, and 10 percent of EFT donors. After the first year, however, the drop-off rate is generally lower, often only half as high as in Year 1.

The method of giving tends to be the single most important factor that influences the rate of attrition in monthly donors, but there are other factors as well. I'll address each of them in turn.

Method by which a donor is recruited

Generally, I find direct mail-recruited donors give longer than those acquired through most other means. However, television-acquired monthly donors recruited by child sponsorship organizations also tend to have a very long life. You need to test different methods and then calculate the Long-Term Value for your cause.

Age of your members

A highly committed, 40-year-old new monthly giving club member may well support your organization every month for the next 40 years. A person who signs up at the age of 70 can't be expected to give that long. Retirement means some people have to stop giving. Ill health or death sometimes also intrudes, of course. So, all other things being equal, younger members may be better than older ones.

However, in the real world we inhabit, things are rarely all equal. For one thing, donors can be too young. Young people's interests are more likely to change, and their financial stability may not be as great. Also, they're not as valuable when you consider the likelihood that a 15-year-donor who dies at the age of 75 is far more likely to leave you a generous legacy.

Quality of your program

If your communications with donors are frequent and meaningful . . . if you listen to what they want—and give it to them . . . they'll remain active donors for a far longer time.

Continued relevance of your program or organization

If your organization loses its relevance, donors will drop off sooner. For instance, if a cure for AIDS were found tomorrow, then AIDS service organizations would see a much higher attrition rate than if the pandemic continues.

Geographic base of your donors

Nonprofits that have smaller service areas will probably find that their donors discontinue giving at a higher rate than do those who support national organizations. (The average North American moves every five years.) For example, the commitment of a member of Bread for the World should remain the same if the donor moves from California to Delaware. But a donor who contributes to a battered women's shelter in San Diego would be more likely to support a shelter in her new community in Delaware.

One organization's attrition rates

Here are the actual figures for one organization.

In one year, out of a base of 6,230 monthly donors, 340 people dropped off. Of this number, 14 percent had died (49 individuals). The total represented a drop-off of just 5.5 percent.

Twenty per cent (68) of the 340 lapsed monthly donors had been enrolled in the program for more than ten years. Their most often-cited reasons for quitting were layoffs and retirement.

Seven of those who lapsed had been contributing at the rate of $150 or more per month. One canceled for four months and intended to return. One was laid off. The other five donors had just retired, so their income was reduced.

Cash flow considerations

Even though you can readily prove on paper that you can raise hundreds of thousands of dollars from a monthly donor program, you may not have strong enough cash flow to build a program rapidly. If it takes six months to break even, and you invest $50,000, can you handle the cash flow? Here's what a simple cash flow chart would look like, with a break-even point at the end of six months.

	Month #1	Month #2	Month #3	Month #4	Month #5	Month #6	Total
Cost	$20K	$12K	$10K	$4K	$2K	$2K	$50K
Revenue	0K	1K	5K	10K	14K	20K	50K
Balance	($20K)	($31K)	($36K)	($30K)	($18K)	($0)	

By your six-month break-even point, let's say that $20,000 of the $50,000 income came from single gifts. So, the monthly giving program itself accounted for $30,000. Let's assume further that, in Month 6, $8,000 of the $20,000 in total income was in the form of single gifts, and $12,000 in monthly gifts. (The latter could consist of $15/month gifts from 800 new monthly donors.)

Now, what happens after the six-month break-even point? For the rest of the year, assuming your program is limited to credit cards and EFT—and taking attrition into account—the cash flow chart might look like this:

	Month #7	Month #8	Month #9	Month #10	Month #11	Month #12	Total
Cost	$2K	$2K	$2K	$2K	$2K	$2K	$62K
Revenue	12K	11.5K	11.5K	11.5K	11K	11K	118.5K
Balance	10K	19.5K	29K	38.5K	47.5K	56.5K	56.5K
Donors	800	767	767	767	767	733	

Note: The "Total" figures on this second chart represent costs and revenue for the entire year.

Over a twelve-month period, your net income is $56,500 ($118,500 - $62,000). But that's only a small part of the value your monthly donors deliver to your organization. With typical rates of attrition and growth, these donors will ultimately contribute another $500,000 to $1 million— and 85 to 95 percent of that will be profit!

AFTERWORD

So, what's the most important contribution made by a monthly giving program? The enhanced Long-Term Value is obviously important. But it's only important because it helps you raise money.

Money is just a tool. A tool to improve our communities and planet.

A few years ago, my filmmaking partner, Peter Davis, and I made a film about a friend, Jon Gates, who died from AIDS. Jon was a tireless human rights advocate and community activist, and he dedicated the last years of his life to fight the impact of AIDS in the developing world.

Just months before his death, Jon gave the keynote address at the Canadian AIDS Society annual conference. In it he said, "I do not have it within my capacity to make those of you who are ill, well. Nor do you collectively have it within your capacity to make me well. But together we can start to make the world well. And at the end of the day, that is one of the primary reasons we are here."

I agree with Jon that together, and only together, can we make the world "well." I thank you for your efforts to make the world a better place and I hope this book contributes to your ability to raise more money, to accomplish the task of building more caring and healthier communities.

How to contact me

I'd love to see your monthly donor materials or find out how your program is working. Who knows, your package may make the 2nd Edition of this book. Thanks for reading this far, and good luck!

Harvey McKinnon
Harvey McKinnon & Associates, Inc.
#218 - 2211 West 4th Avenue
Vancouver, Canada, BC V6K 4S2
phone: 1-800-815-8565 / e-mail: Harveym@direct.ca

APPENDIX 1
Guide to Illustrations

APPENDIX 2
Recommended Reading & Resources

Books

999 Tips, Trends and Guidelines for Successful Direct Mail and Telephone Fundraising, Mal Warwick with Deborah Block, Stephen Hitchcock, Ivan Levison, and Joseph H. White, Jr., Strathmoor Press, Berkeley, CA.

The Art of Asking Properly, George Smith, White Lion Press, London.

Dear Friend: Mastering the Art of Direct Mail Fundraising, Kay Partney Lautman and Henry Goldstein, FRI Institute, Maryland.

Direct Mail Testing for Fundraisers, Joseph Kachorek, Precept Press, Illinois.

Direct Marketing, Ed Nash, McGraw Hill, New York.

Direct Response Television, Frank R. Brady and Angel Vasquez, NTC Business Books, Illinois.

First Things First, Steven R. Covey, Simon and Schuster, New York.

Friends for Life: Relationship Fundraising in Practice, Ken Burnett, White Lion Press, London.

How to Write a Fundraising Letter, Conrad Squires, Precept Press, Illinois.

Sacred Cows Make the Best Burgers, Robert Krieger, Warner Books, New York.

Seven Habits of Highly Effective People, Steven R. Covey, Simon and Schuster, New York.

Successful Direct Marketing Methods, Bob Stone, NTC Business Books, Illinois.

The Successful Volunteer Organization, Getting Started and Getting Results in Non-Profit, Charitable, Grassroots and Community Groups, Joan Flanagan, Contemporary Books, Inc., Illinois.

Type & Layout, Colin Wheildon with foreword by David Ogilvy, Strathmoor Press, Berkeley, CA

Periodicals

Canadian Fundraiser, The Hillborn Group Ltd., Toronto, Canada

Direct, Cowles Business Media, Inc., Stamford, CT.

Direct Marketing Magazine, Hoke Communications, Inc., New Jersey

Fundraising Management, Hoke Communications, Inc., New Jersey

Response TV, Advanstar Communications, Santa Ana, CA.

Successful Direct Mail & Telephone Fundraising, Strathmoor Press, Berkeley, CA.

Target Marketing, North American Publishing Co., Philadelphia, PA.

Telemarketing, Technology Marketing Corporation, CT.

Who's Mailing What!, North American Publishing Co., Philadelphia, PA.

Videos

Friends for Life: The Video Series, Harvey McKinnon Productions, 1997. Vancouver, Canada. (800) 815-8565

How to Build a Highly Successful Monthly Donor Program, Harvey McKinnon Productions, 1997. Vancouver, Canada. (800) 815-8565

Secrets of Successful Fundraisers, Harvey McKinnon Productions, 1997.

Vancouver, Canada. (800) 815-8565

APPENDIX 3
EFT Service Providers

CHI Cash Advance
325 S. Highland Avenue
Briarcliff Manor
NY 10510
212-862-0500
888-CHI-0500
914-923-0500
www.chi-cash-advance.com

EFT Corporation
2911 Dixwell Avenue
Hamden, CT 06518
(800) 338-2435
www.etransfer.com
email: eft@etransfer.com

FINET (Financial Electronic Transfer, Inc.)
500 W. Lincoln Trail Box 998
Radcliff, KY 40159-0988
(800) 351-1239
502-351-1919
www.gopay.com

Payment Solutions
P.O. Box 30217
Bethesda, MD 20824
(301) 986-1062

Beacon Financial Group, Inc.
1501 Commerce Avenue
Carlise, PA 17013
(717) 249-8800
1-800-DO-DEBIT
www.bfgi.com
email: info@bfgi.com

INDEX

About the Author

Harvey McKinnon, CFRE is internationally recognized as an expert on building monthly donor programs. As a consultant, he has helped hundreds of U.S. and Canadian nonprofits to successfully launch and expand monthly giving programs. An entertaining and highly rated trainer and speaker, Harvey has lectured on five continents. This is his first book.